THE FALCONER

THE FALCONER

WHAT WE WISH WE HAD LEARNED IN SCHOOL

A PRIMER FOR 21ST CENTURY EDUCATION

Grant Lichtman

iUniverse, Inc.
New York   Bloomington

The Falconer
What We Wish We Had Learned in School

iUniverse books may be ordered through booksellers or by contacting:

iUniverse
1663 Liberty Drive
Bloomington, IN 47403
www.iuniverse.com
1-800-Authors (1-800-288-4677)

ISBN: 978-1-4502-3126-8 (sc)
ISBN: 978-1-4502-3127-5 (ebk)

Printed in the United States of America

iUniverse rev. date: 05/13/2010

Dedication

The students of The Falconer classes 1999–2003 of Francis Parker School, San Diego, are some of the most remarkably thoughtful, creative, and visionary young people I have ever met. I hope that in some cases our discussions had a fraction of the impact on their lives and thought processes that they had on mine.

Contents

Acknowledgments

This book is the result of conversations, trials, and testing in the classroom ranging over a period of more than twenty years. No doubt I will have forgotten many whose thoughts and input have contributed to the final product, but I hope that the following list comprises most who deserve special note, though not blame, for the model that has evolved.

The students of The Falconer seminar are first in line for thanks. Over a period of five years, more than eighty high school students at Francis Parker School gave up lunch and study times to participate in a college-level course for which most received no credit on their transcript. They gambled that the experience would be worthwhile, and for the most part, I believe, it was. They have gone on to college, graduate programs, and successful careers.

W. Lee Pierson, former headmaster of Francis Parker School, gave me the opportunity to teach this remarkable group of students the first year. Carol Obermeier and Chris Harrington, members of the English faculty at Parker, sat in on a number of seminars, and Ms. Obermeier reviewed and edited a draft of the manuscript. Robert Landis, former student, also reviewed the manuscript and provided substantive comments. Michael Moreno, former student, reviewed the manuscript and provided probably the most compelling reason for me to move forward and publish when he called from the Green Zone in Baghdad and said that he really wanted the Falconer model at hand in a book that he could reach for in time of need. Kevin Yaley allowed me to team teach with him in order to refine some of the subject matter within a broader context of his philosophy and ethics course. Daniel Stuessy, founder and owner of Opterra, Inc., was my coauthor on a series of articles related to alternate dispute resolution that developed the "getting ahead of no" model for proactively seeking solutions to problems before they occur. Brad Lichtman, Dana Shelbourne, and Ted Tibbs are all educators in the San Diego area, and it was discussions with them more than twenty years ago that led to the concept that great teaching arises from leading students to find, not solve, problems in the classroom. Ben Malayang is currently president of Silliman University, Dumaguete City, Philippines, where I taught for a year in 1981 and formulated a number of the concepts of systems analysis while working with Mr. Malayang and others at the Silliman Environmental Center.

The Falconer class and this book draw on the classic book of strategy, *The Art of War* by Sun Tzu, of which there are a number of available translations and interpretations. All direct quotes from *The Art of War* included in this book have been drawn from the 2007 edition published by J.W. Edwards, Inc. and Borders Classics. Permission to use these quotes has been graciously granted and facilitated by J. W. Edwards, Borders Classics and the Ann Arbor Media Group (see References and Suggested Readings for the full reference). For teachers, students, and readers interested in further study of *The Art of War*, this edition is recommended for its clarity, ease of use, and availability.

Introduction

School prepares us to be successful. We aspire to be happy.
Robert Landis, Falconer Class of 2001

We are not teaching our children, our students, and our co-workers what they really need to know. The lessons aren't out there on some shelf or Web site. They won't be found with more money and more programs to push more stuff in more different ways at our kids and our employees. It's not about computer-to-student ratios, distance learning, high-speed links to the Library of Congress, or lecture podcasts. It's not a pricey self-help guru claiming that his "new thing" is new, seven cookbook steps to success, or ten simple mileposts to make a million for your company.

Those tools help, but they are the dressing, like ornaments on a Christmas tree. We need to pay attention to the tree itself. Look at the people who *invented* computers, who *designed* the Internet, who *overcame* the Depression, who *envisioned* the best sellers, who *challenged* racism, who *explored* the ocean depths, who *built* the Panama Canal, who *created* the management-consulting firms that you hire to tell you how to run your business more efficiently. I want my children and my employees and my co-workers and my friends to exhibit qualities like invention, courage, creativity, insight, design, and vision a lot more than I want them to know the capitals of South America or the sequence of presidents and kings, fractions, computer science, art history, running a cash register, or throwing a football.

In short, I want us to spend more time teaching how to generate and recognize elegant solutions to the many problems facing our world.

Why in our great system of child rearing and primary, secondary, college, graduate, and postgraduate education is there no course of study titled something like Strategies for Becoming Who I Want to Be? Is it that our vast machine of education and training, so finely crafted in the industrial and postindustrial age to turn out competent, productive, knowledgeable, and efficient cogs, just hasn't gotten around to it yet? Is it that the search for elegance should be reserved for geniuses? Is there a step in the life-long process of learning that we have overlooked or hidden which can transcend the teaching of competency and knowledge, which can provide us with the

1

additional tools of creation, invention, and wisdom? Can we actually teach these strategies from an early age?

Come along and see.

On this journey, we will ask many, many questions and find some answers, but one thing we accept at the outset is that we never find *valuable* answers without searching for them. That's what real journeys are all about, so be prepared to work a little. Remember Dorothy in Oz? She had the answer all along, but she needed to walk a long road, to overcome humbugs, tornadoes, burning brooms, falling houses, and flying monkeys before her belief in the power of friendship and family showed her the way home. There are just some things that no Good Witch or teacher or boss or parent can discover for us; we have to learn it for ourselves.

I am not alone at the forefront of those calling for a change in how we view the priorities of education and training. Visionary educational leaders agree that we need to teach our students and employees to be more creative, to search for the unknown, to redouble their efforts in the face of failure, to bridge the gaps between disciplines in order to invent. What is perhaps new is that we have actually *done it*. We have created and tested a teaching model with stories and examples that work at the high school and even elementary level. We have taken that first important step of proving that this type of education is both possible and practical. You will find the model and the stories in this book.

Who is this book for? The teachers and students in all of us. Learning takes place in schools and colleges and professional training centers when *every one of us* is either a student or teacher or both. Business leaders learn from their mentors, their investors, and the harsh gods of the market place, and they have a vital need to educate both their employees and their customers. Parents have learned the lessons of their own youth and try to pass those keys along to their children, often in a world where the shape of the locks has changed. We think of children as the ultimate learners, absorbing lessons as they grow, and then in their innocence and with their unique youthful perceptions, they become the instructor.

So who is this book for? It is for all of us who encounter the ultimate task master every day: a life that can ensnare us in tangled brambles, throw us a greasy curveball, jump out at us in the middle of a dark night from behind the closet door when no one else is home. But it is also a life that brings us orange and coral sunsets over a flat lavender sea, Beethoven's Sixth over coffee on Sunday, babies who grow up and graduate with honors, and the ceiling of the Sistine Chapel. This book is for those of us who want to avoid more of the brambles and enjoy more of the sunsets.

A central theme of this book is the critical importance of asking questions, and one of the first questions that *I* would ask at the start of a thought journey is "Who am I listening to?" Let me introduce myself.

At various times in my adult life, I have been a scientist, entrepreneur, student, teacher, builder, writer, reader, husband, businessman (generally successful), traveler, and father. After twelve years of public primary and secondary education, six years of undergraduate and graduate work at the University of California and Stanford, and more than fifteen years in business, I asked myself what I had learned that I wished someone had taught me in high school but didn't. I wrote an outline while lying on the couch one afternoon and turned that outline into a seminar course that I taught for five years at a small high school in San Diego, California. We proved that we can overtly teach young people to be more creative, strategic, and inventive in their thinking, to make the leap from a passive learner of previous knowledge to an active creator of new ideas. You will find some of my students' thoughts sprinkled throughout the book. Do they sound wise and prophetic beyond their tender years? Yes, but they were just seventeen-year-old kids who gave up their lunch times for a no-credit seminar and the chance to ask a lot of, and about, themselves.

On any journey it is useful to have guides. We will employ a number, both real and mythical, as their unique expertise is required. The real ones are friends, authors, and students who, over the years, have given me some precious nugget of clarity that made me want to slap my forehead and smile and say, "Yes, now I get it!" The made-up guides are convenient provocateurs who, like Dorothy's Good Witch, will help us towards our own self-discovery. Why so many guides? Why not one leader at the head of the trail who tells us when to turn and what to look at and where to stand to get the best snapshot? Should not a fundamental truth be simple and easy to see, like "E=mc^2," "buy low and sell high," or "never draw to an inside straight"? But like a kaleidoscope or a glass bead game or the feathery twirls of Chaos, there are multiple paths through the mosaic, and our guides each have a particular role to play as the paths unfold.

One of our principle guides may be *both* real and fictional. *The Art of War* is one of the most studied and interpreted manuscripts in the history of the world, yet its credited author, Sun Tzu, remains a controversial mystery, perhaps a single author, perhaps a group of scholars. As Mr. Sun will tell us when we meet him, he is surprised that, with all of the standard interpretations of his work related to war and business and conflict and martial arts, no one yet has studied the obvious connection to the pursuit of personal happiness. *The Falconer* weaves the ancient text and this new interpretation together in a way that even my high school students found clear, compelling, and helpful. Who better to act as our principle guide and commentator than Sun Tzu himself, or at least some convenient versions of him?

This book is not a direct path; few problems in life are clean and linear, so why should our solutions be more so? Here are three explicit points that may help the reader as the paths of this journey grow and cross:

1. We all learn by experience better than by instruction. Since the thought journey *is* the experience, there are sections that may not make sense until placed within the context of a later chapter; you just have to have a little faith. But since this book may be used as a text as well as a popular guide, I have extracted key items and placed them in an appendix in the back, the Cheat Sheets. Use them as needed, but like skimming *Cliff's Notes* instead of reading *Moby Dick*, a lot will be lost if used alone.

2. There are two parallel stories here. One major thesis of this book is that the central tenets of strategic and creative thinking are simple enough to teach to a small child. One of the story lines, that of Mr. Usher and the Children, therefore, is written in a *Winnie the Pooh* language that even elementary children can understand. I know because I gave these chapters to my own kids when they were that age and they "got it." This does not mean that the lessons of this story line are inapplicable to adult situations. Far from it. But for those of you who are parents and teachers, who want to help your youngsters get a head start on these lessons, feel free to tear the Mr. Usher chapters out of the book and give them to your young charges. For the older reader, the Mr. Usher chapters will weave together with the more adult-level sections and hopefully make the path more enjoyable for the children in all of us.

3. Please do not worry about the seemingly separate identities of our guides, Sun Tzu (who we refer to as Mr. Sun) and Sunny. They are one and the same, two reflections of the same voice. They are both helping us to convert ancient wisdom into simple and easily applicable pathways of strategic thinking. They come and go also in a nonlinear fashion as we need them, and in the end you will be comfortable with their habit of popping in and out of the lessons as needed.

Most of this journey will be comfortable, like a warm bed on a fall evening, tea and crumpets at five, a gentle stroll, a flat-green three-foot putt. At some point, though, we have to pay the price of our assumptions, of our deliberate arrogance, for setting the bar high. The world is sometimes cruel, and we can't apologize for that; we need to look underground as well as to the heavens. There will come a time when all the theory and stories and hope just won't hold the weight. By that time we pray we have learned and trusted the tools that will allow us to read on, to climb out of the hole, and still have our wholeness. But that is up to each of us. We will test this mettle, without which our path is just a fairy tale. The search for elegance if rarely a smooth curve or a straight line.

So let's go; our guides await. The nearest convenient stepping-in point is at the edge of a dewy meadow, and it is cold.

The Path Starts in a Meadow

We would all trade a lot of knowledge for a little bit of wisdom.
Aaron Butler, Falconer Class of 1998

Heavy morning dew blankets the brown, bent grass of a wide meadow. A wreath of alder and pine edges the meadow, broken only by the trail we have recently walked. Cold mist slowly dissolves in front of the low, winter sun. We hear the muffled creak of harness leather and horses' hooves drumming slowly on the damp earth. Three horses and their riders melt out of the mist, steam rushing from the horses' nostrils at each breath. The riders are shielded from the foggy cold by medieval layers of heavy gray leggings and thick woolen coats. The tallest rider holds his left arm bent at the elbow; his right hand grasps the reins. The mist seems to part and form up again as the small cavalry makes its way at a stately walk to the center of the dewy glade.

The three riders part company. Two dismount and hand their reins to the third, who takes the horses, ties them at the edge of the forest, and stands beneath a thick pine, half burnt from a prehistoric lightning strike. We watch the other two, a grown man and a young boy. The boy sets his bundles on the ground and moves away, squatting in the wet grass, watching intently the moves of his teacher. The teacher drives a stake into the ground and directs the hooded falcons onto it, tying their thin leather leg traces to the stake. Only then does he look about himself at the conditions of the meadow and forest, the mist slowly lifting like curtains before a play, a few cautious songbirds trilling in the trees following the passage of strangers. The birth of a breeze bends the tops of the tallest pine. He tests the dampness of the soil with his boot, sniffs some far-off scent like a hunting dog, and waits.

The falconer has learned his art over many years, starting as a young apprentice, no older than the assistant who now squats and watches nearby. His art is a braid of elastic perceptions of when his raptors are willing, how and when the trainer is successful, when the forest and meadows are cooperative, and when the falconer wishes sport or needs meat for his table. The inevitable consequence of a successful flight is violence and blood; the need should warrant the result. What distillation proceeds in the mind of the falconer in the meadow, before and after? Why do we care?

The falconer has, over the lives of his birds, each day, in the morning before flight, carefully assessed the strengths and weaknesses of each falcon. They are his essential tools. Without them and his understanding of them, he is a shackled tourist enjoying naught but a cold morning with his horse. He has chosen this meadow and forest over all other meadows and forests on this particular morning. He has led his trusting assistants out of their warm beds, and success or failure rests primarily on his judgment. The table, if this is a day of provisioning, will be full or not based on his knowledge and application of the art.

Should he fly the birds while the masking mist conceals their attack, or when their vision to the target is unimpaired? Can he control both birds in flight at once, and what would happen if wild raptors intercede? Is the prey abundant or elusive? Does the pigeon need to die today? The braid is thick with questions, which the falconer weighs on a balance of calculation and valuation.

The assistant carefully takes note of his teacher's deliberation, learning the skills that will lead the youngster to his own goals, whatever they might be.

*   *   *   *

We turn our heads, you and I, the observers of this opening act, and look into the corner office of a downtown high-rise, its mirrored windows bouncing reflections back and forth with the skyscraper across the street. In the office, two women sit on opposite sides of a polished table heaped with papers and folders and computer printouts. The tapping of calculators, the soft hum of a hard drive, and the scraping of their pencils heighten the edge of tension.

A mélange of colorful charts and graphs with the names of companies and product lines cascade along one wall like military units on a battle plan. The women work relentlessly, check and recheck their numbers against those on the charts, unwilling to leave to chance the one minuscule item that may sink their hopes of a profitable merger. The length and intensity of their labor is recorded in the hysteria of coffee cups and sandwich bags piled in a corner trashcan.

These women have tuned their business skills for years, in school and on the street. They have become accustomed to the frightening risks and the dizzying rewards, failing as often as they have succeeded. They learned a long time ago that failure is usually a better teacher, though a more painful one. But with each year and each venture, their skills have grown and their strategies have sharpened.

An assistant enters the office and drops off yet another batch of printouts. He leaves and the two women glance grimly at each other. If the merger is successful, this young man will have a job next month. If not, he won't. In their skills lies the assistant's immediate future. If their vision is sound, the assistant will thank them profusely as his stock options inflate. If their vision is faulty, he will damn them from the halls of some other office building or from the unemployment line.

Is the timing right? Are the financials sound? Is their backing solid? Will the employees cooperate? Will the union agree to renegotiate its contract? Can the women make the financial markets see their own clear vision of the combined strength and flexibility of these two heretofore corporate antagonists? Their heads drop again to the numbers, because the time for questioning and understanding is past and the time for action falls tomorrow with the gavel of the shareholders' meeting.

Will they succeed? They don't know but they will try.

*   *   *   *

We turn our heads again and look down on a city park where broad oak trees shed their autumn leaves around the edge of a brown grass knoll. At the end of a rutted dirt footpath, two picnic benches have been pulled together end to end. A group of young men, boys really, crowd the benches. They flex their shoulders and lock predatory eyes across the table. We see and hear them pound their fists and shout angrily, drowning each other out in a caustic stew of accusation and obscenity. The boys all come from the same neighborhood, but their tattoos and colors distinguish one group as the enemies of the other. The anger at the tables overwhelms the autumn afternoon.

A middle-aged man, dressed in black except for the white collar of his faith, stands at one end of the tables. His hands are raised over the boys in pleading supplication, trying to dampen the shouts and still the fists. We try, but can't hear his pleas for calm. Slowly, the shouting recedes; the priest takes a deep breath, looking about himself for strength, and the cross-table glares sputter and flare.

For years the priest has sought another path from conflict, a substitute for destructive discord, a way to create parallel victory out of coincidental defeat. The combatants come before him, or he seeks them out, the husbands and wives who suffer the perceived prison of their respective lives; the fractious apartment dwellers who seethe at the disrespect of their neighbors; the haughty, self-righteous gangbangers who now sit with him in the park, posturing to preserve their dignity before sacrificing their friends to the shotgun and the Uzi. Each time the priest tries to help them craft a path that will lead them to success instead of failure. God told him that the peacemakers are blessed, but he has had to learn how and why on his own. He has learned the patient tools of observation, perception, and persuasion that, sometimes, help him help his petitioners.

Acorns fall from the shading oak more quickly than the two groups of boys agree to the smallest of resolutions, but they do start to agree. Gently, slowly, the mediator- priest steers each side a whisper closer to resolution and a step further from battle. So many questions remain, and the sun is already behind the tenements on the west side of the park. Will they come back tomorrow? How many of them will see dawn from the inside of the emergency room? Is patience alone a sharp enough tool to excise the tumors of hate and jealousy? Is there an end, or just an intermission to this deadly play? How can he help them when he can only partly see what they see?

At dusk the boys get up to leave, swaggering away from the table as if to prove they've left nothing behind; one turns around and smiles at the priest, and then quickly turns away in case his hope is illusionary.

*   *   *   *

We are suddenly distracted by the noise of running water, a cheery, babbling that is out of place in the urban park. We turn once more and look into a high mountain meadow. The sun is setting over steep peaks to the west, casting long, chilly shadows across the rangy grass and a small group of children who stand facing a wall of rock. In the middle of the children is a lone adult, facing the rock as well. The small brook whose tumble attracted us wanders through the meadow, past the children, and down a long valley to the south. A footpath parallels the stream, and it is at the intersection of this path and the sheer rock face that the group now stands. We can hear their discussion:

"Well, you're certainly right," says the teacher. "The trail has stopped. What do *you* suggest we do?"

"*We* don't know what to do," a boy answers. "You're the teacher. Tell us where to go."

"We've never been here before," adds a young girl. "How are *we* supposed to know which way to go?"

"I'm ready for your suggestions," says the teacher. "I'm not at all sure that there *is* any one best way to proceed here. Who has a good idea about what to do?"

The talk fades against the sound of the running water, as the small group talks and points and discusses how they will extricate themselves from their dead end. Finally, they decide to spend the night in the meadow and try the mountain the next day. They roll out their sleeping bags, kindle a small fire, and huddle around it in the black mountain night. Some look worriedly up at the shadows of the mountain in front of them.

"I suggest we all get some sleep," says the teacher. "Remember, when you're looking for an answer, all paths may look equally good, but they rarely are. Think and sleep on it, and tomorrow we'll try to find a way over the mountain."

The children go off to their sleeping bags and tents, and the teacher sits with the dying embers, thinking about the days' lessons and what to do in the morning. He has brought his children so far, not just on this trip, but also over several years as their teacher. Now they are facing a *real* problem, not just a theory he has constructed on the blackboard. How will they respond? Will they use the tools he has tried to provide? Has he given them enough? What might happen on the mountain the next day that he has not foreseen? Is this too much of an adventure- problem for his young charges? How can he combine the fire of experience with the knowledge of his lesson without endangering his students?

The teacher ponders by the fire until the coals die out, trying to plan the future, hoping that there is more than one path leading out of the meadow.

*　　　*　　　*　　　*

We are torn away from the idyllic mountain night to the harsh glare of overhead lights, white walls, and aluminum desks, and the industrial hum of computers, displays, disk drives, and line printers echoing through a windowless cave that may be high above the street or deep below ground. All time is work time here.

Stern young faces scan the screens in front of them as pictures, videos, tables, and text scroll by at the touch of a mouse. The operators all are plugged in with tiny voice mikes and invisible earpieces; they almost whisper into their respective domains, looking, pondering, commenting, listening, moving vast puzzles of seemingly disparate information on and off of their electronic consoles, occasionally rubbing their eyes, reading hard copy, making a note, shredding a stack.

They are the puzzle masters, both owner and slave to the information matrix of a modern world. They are tasked with sifting through the common detritus of an electronic society, looking for a one-in-a-million connection that may, just may, point the direction towards bad people doing bad things. Every one of them will fail a thousand times for every time they succeed. They will make the wrong assessment a thousand times for every time they are right. They will implicate innocent people a thousand times for every time they find the guilty. They will have to ask a thousand questions for every meaningful answer.

Have we found every piece of the puzzle that can be found? Have we sorted the data in meaningful ways? Have we asked the questions that no one else dared to ask? Have we thought beyond the boundaries of our own training, upbringing, and worldview? Have we created a link that did not exist before we came along, just in time? If so, then just once, someone will find a connection that no one else has seen; will match information in a new place and in a new way; will visualize the invisible just one step ahead of the terrorist cell that is bent on useless destruction, and unbeknownst to just about all of the rest of us, a disaster will have been averted.

The puzzle masters listen and sift, watch and create, often ignorant of their successes and failures.

*   *   *   *

Our final turn into a summer evening shows us the living room of a suburban home, yellow light streaming out of tall gabled windows onto a dark, manicured garden. A mother and father sit rigidly on the sofa while, sprawled defiantly across an easy chair, their teenage daughter plays with her long, straight hair and tries to create a dimension in which her parents don't exist. The dishwasher running in the kitchen and a computer game squawking upstairs only amplify the silence when the parents stop speaking. The carpet is clean, but the paths from the kitchen and bedrooms into this living area are worn by the passage of a family.

For years the parents have gleaned the art of parenting as the children grew, learning from books and television and newspapers and friends. They have dredged out every memory of their own youth and have tried to remember what worked and why. Their love for their children is overwhelming, but now they face the shock that love may not be enough. Their beloved daughter is ignoring them.

First it was the boyfriend, then the tattered pants, then the mess of a room, and each time their daughter argued their rules as if the United Nations itself cared nothing for her human rights. Then mom found the single rolled joint shoved into her daughter's dresser drawer (far less than mom and dad had hidden at that age, but a dramatic escalation of defiance nonetheless), and all that their daughter would say was that if they didn't understand they just didn't love her.

How do they argue this? How can she question their love? When, between physics and math and English and history, when, between jobs and diapers and paying bills, were they supposed to learn how to untie this kind of knot? What do parents have left when our children doubt our love? Which battles do they fight and which do they leave alone, and if they leave any of them alone, are they bad parents, baiting their children to turn into disrespectful, unsuccessful hangers-on?

On the upper landing of the stairs, hidden but straining to hear every word, the younger sister listens and studies the one-sided conversation below. She knows her parents love them and can't fathom that someday she, too, will throw the same question into her parents' faces.

*   *   *   *

We turn again and look back over our shoulder to see what has made a soft scraping sound. A middle-aged man dressed in flowing scarlet robes of ancient Chinese silk is watching us view the scenes around us. He has taken notes of each diorama and of us as we witnessed them. There is something familiar about him, as if we have seen him a long time ago, or maybe in a dream encrusted with the telling. A sword lies by his side, but it is rusty and clearly has not been used for years. His pen, however, is sharp. We find that, unlike the other scenes we have passively observed, we can talk to him. We introduce ourselves, and he bows courteously. He says his name is Sun Tzu. We ask Mr. Sun if we have ever met him or dreamt of him before as he looks familiar to us. He nods, yes, and points back to where the falconer still stands in the meadow, the sun having burned off the morning mist and dried the grass. The falconer's arm is raised, and the first bird of the day is streaking skyward after an unseen prey. But we don't watch the falconer or the bird because we recognize a young Sun Tzu, the apprentice, carefully taking note of the art of falconing, learning the patience and virtues and skills his master displays.

Mr. Sun motions for us to follow him. He sits on a bench and takes out a faded manuscript, hand-printed in black characters on fragile rice paper.

"I hope you are not disconcerted by the apparent time gap here," he says. "I've been dead for a couple of millennia, but let's not allow that to get in the way. I wrote a simple book a long time ago, and many people in your time still read it. I used the language of war and the warrior to convey my ideas about how to face and overcome personal challenges, how to use the tools that we each posses in order to face and solve problems, how to take advantage of opportunities. Sometimes these challenges and problems and opportunities involve war and conflict, or business, economics, and the pursuit of profit but more often they do not. Usually my ideas apply to one person, deciding how to go forward in life in order to increase his or her happiness and that of those around them."

We tell Mr. Sun that we are indeed familiar with his book, and that it is taught in business schools and war colleges and martial arts *dojos* as a tool of great strategic insight. He nods and looks down at the rice paper.

"That is all well and good, but why make the simple complicated? Why teach to just business people and generals what we might more easily teach to moms, dads, and children? I think if people understood the language that I used, understood what I mean by war and warrior, they might see that my ideas are good for more than fighting an enemy in war, competing in business, or overcoming an opponent in the martial arts."

We tell Mr. Sun that we could not agree with him more, and we ask him how we might help.

"I am not interested only in battles where people die and armies annihilate each other. Unfortunately, these conflicts arise, and in my time and part of the world, armed conflict was even more prevalent than it is today. I am much more interested in how we each can better create, learn, teach, lead, motivate, envision, and decide the future of our lives. Perhaps from time to time I can interrupt your observations with some of my own, and we can discuss what I *really* meant in my book."

We respond that, of course, we would be honored to have him watch over our shoulders as we proceed and to insert his commentary and guidance at any point. We're not entirely sure what he means to do, but contribution from such a revered poet of strategy is priceless.

Mr. Sun gives us the old manuscript and tells us that if and when we come to a passage that seems particularly relevant to our current topic, to take note, and he will be happy to help us understand his meaning. We take the rice paper and note happily that the Chinese characters have melted away, and we can read the modern translation very nicely. We tuck the paper away, and thank Mr. Sun for his help, assuring him that we shall call upon him frequently.

Mr. Sun motions us to go on with our work, and turns back to watch his younger self fidget in the cold of an ancient Chinese meadow while his master concentrates on the falcons, streaking across the sky.

By looking at the end of several trails, we have found the place to start.

Step -1: Who Do I Want to Be?

The answers to who we are can be found in the questions we dare to ask.
Chantal Blakeney, Falconer Class of 2004

We are selling our children short when we believe that grappling is beyond them. In fact, most of them are engaging in dilemmas of intense seriousness while we are looking the other way.
Sizer and Sizer, *The Students are Watching*

We have now met the first of our guides, the ancient Chinese warrior-philosopher Sun Tzu. It is not clear if a single author is responsible for *The Art of War* or if it is an amalgam of thoughts produced by a school of similarly minded scholars. We do know that *The Art of War* has been analyzed, prodded, pondered, discussed, translated, reprinted, taught, and wrestled with as much as any nonreligious text in the history of the world. We also know that it is not really about war. It is startling in its simplicity, which makes Mr. Sun and his clean, concise imagery such valuable touchstones along our path. Our challenge is to make the trials of personal strategy and the pursuit of happiness just as simple. What we will find as we match the language of our model to that of *The Art of War* is remarkable congruence and simplicity of metaphor and message. We will meet with Mr. Sun frequently as we identify specific passages of *The Art of War* that clearly pertain to personal strategic planning.

We are now ready to meet our second guide. Since our path is founded on the process of learning, who better to follow than a mythical teacher and his flock of students. Theirs is the business of learning, and to prove to ourselves that the path is not overly difficult, we will make the students young. We will challenge our teacher to create lessons that are so simple that even a young child may follow.

Since all paths must progress, we will take one liberty with our teacher and his students: they get to stay together in their respective roles year after year. They get to know and trust each other over time, and their lessons grow with them. They walk this path together from beginning to end. This may not reflect the reality of our own schools and training centers, but that's what myths are for.

Allow me to introduce you to Mr. Usher and the Children.

$*$ $*$ $*$ $*$

The Lesson of Heroes

In our mythical little valley, the school year starts the first week of September, when the days are still long and hot, and it feels as if summer will never end. I'm sure it's the same for you each year; you get that tingling of sadness that another summer vacation is gone, mixed with excitement about seeing your friends in school again. Each year, back we go, though it always seems to take a few weeks, and maybe an autumn rain or two, before all of the students stop gazing out the window in the middle of the day, wishing they were back fishing by a lazy creek or playing baseball in the evening after supper.

The year Mr. Usher came to his school September was a glorious splash of warm days and still evenings. The big old oak tree in the schoolyard was so full of acorns that the squirrels couldn't begin to hide all of them away before winter. The school gardener had cut the grass in the schoolyard the day before class started, and the neat lawn made the whole school smell like the middle of July. The sun still rises early in September in the valley, and the grass was dry of dew by the time the children came running into the yard on that first day of class.

When the morning bell rang, the students all lined up in front of their classes, just as they did every day for every class. The Children looked nervously down the hall towards the school office. Just as the line was filled, around the corner came a new teacher, and all of the Children knew that this must be Mr. Usher.

Mr. Usher was tall and thin and had a full head of gray hair. He wore a checkered shirt, a plain blue tie, and a worn, comfortable-looking jacket. His glasses rode low on his nose as if they might fall off at any moment. He wasn't too young and wasn't too old. As Mr. Usher approached the head of the line, the first students started to walk into the classroom. Mr. Usher raised his hand and stopped them.

"It's such a beautiful morning, why not stay outside for a while?" he asked, looking over the students in their line. "Let's all sit down over there under the big oak tree and let summer last another few minutes, shall we?"

The Children didn't know what to make of *that*. They'd never heard of a teacher wanting to make summer last any longer, and certainly the other teachers didn't send students out to the schoolyard on the morning of the first day of school. But Mr. Usher walked off towards the big oak tree without looking back, so the Children followed, still more or less lined up. In a few minutes, the Children and Mr. Usher were all seated on the cool grass under the big oak tree, and for once the squirrels stopped their busy chatter, and the robins sat quietly in the high branches or flew off to look for worms in the field out beyond the schoolyard fence.

"First things first," said Mr. Usher. "I'm Mr. Usher, though I imagine you all guessed *that*. Now I need to know who is who among you." So they went around the circle, each student saying his or her name, and Mr. Usher repeated each name under his breath. Soon Mr. Usher knew almost all of the Children's names, though as happens in any new class, I imagine he was still making mistakes for the next few days.

"Welcome to the new school year to all of you," Mr. Usher began. "As you know, I'm new at the school, so I'm sure I have a lot to learn this year, just like you. For a teacher, deciding what to teach, and how, is not as easy as some of you might think. So if you don't mind, I'd like a little bit of help."

Several of the students looked across the circle at each other with their faces screwed up in confusion. Usually on the first day of school, the teachers told the students what they were going to study during the year. *This* new teacher was asking *them* to help *him* decide what to teach. But no one raised a hand to ask Mr. Usher why he needed their help; perhaps because it was the first day of school and all of the Children were a little shy of the tall stranger.

Mr. Usher took a large pad of notepaper out from under his loose jacket and leaned back against the old oak tree. "I want each of you to think of at least one person who you really respect, someone you admire. It can be a real person, or a pretend person, like someone in a story or a movie. It can be someone you know, like a friend or a sister, or someone you don't. This person can be alive or dead. It doesn't matter. I want to know who it is and why you admire this person. Let's all take a few minutes and think about it." And with that, Mr. Usher leaned farther back against the dry bark of the oak tree and began to doodle on his notepad.

The Children all looked at each other and hunched up their shoulders, and no one said a word. It was, after all, a rather unusual request and didn't seem to have anything to do with helping Mr. Usher decide what to teach them that year. A few of the Children whispered to each other, and finally Morgan timidly raised her hand, wondering if Mr. Usher would see it.

"Yes, Morgan, what is it?" asked Mr. Usher, so quickly that you would have thought he was looking right at her over the top of his glasses even before she had raised her hand.

"Excuse me, but I was just wondering, is it all right if we talk to each other about this? Maybe it will help some of us remember who the people are that are important to us."

Mr. Usher smiled at Morgan and then around at all of the Children. "First of all, Morgan, you never have to excuse yourself for asking a question in my class. Rule Number One in my class is that questions are much more important than answers. And yes, of course you may talk about it with each other. Rule Number Two is that anything worth knowing is certainly worth talking about." Mr. Usher smiled again at the Children and went back to doodling on his notepad.

The Children put their heads together in groups of threes and fours and talked quietly for a few minutes sharing ideas and asking each other who they respected or admired and why. After a while the group grew quiet and still, and Mr. Usher looked up from his notepad.

"Let's start at this side of the circle," he said, pointing to his right. "Tell us, Andy, who is it that you respect or admire, and why?"

"Well, last year we studied about a person who tried to fly all the way around the world before any other woman had done it. She didn't make it and no one knows what happened to her, but I want to be a pilot when I grow up, so I guess I admire her. Her name was Amelia Earhart."

"Oh, yes, a very fine choice," smiled Mr. Usher. "And what exactly is it about Amelia Earhart that you admire, other than the fact that she was a pilot? There are many pilots in the world. What is it that makes you think of her as being particularly special?"

Andy frowned and thought for a minute. "Everyone thought she couldn't do it, but she wanted to try something really hard. Even if she didn't make it all the way around the world, she gave it her best try. She believed in herself."

Mr. Usher nodded his head slowly, thinking about what Andy had said. "So you admire her for her self-confidence, is that it?" Mr. Usher asked.

"That's the word I was looking for, self-confidence," said Andy. "That's what I meant when I said Amelia Earhart believed in herself."

Mr. Usher took out a pencil and wrote for a moment on his pad, then looked up at the next student in the circle and raised his eyebrows.

"I respect my father," said Felisa. "It's not just because I love him and he loves me. He's just so helpful whenever I need something. It's not like he does all my work for me or anything like that, but when I need help he's always there, and I think helping other people is very important."

Mr. Usher nodded and wrote on his note pad, and then waved at the next student in line to take his turn. And so they went around the circle until each of the Children had told Mr. Usher whom it was that they respected or admired and why, and all the while Mr. Usher took notes on his pad and smiled at each Child in turn. Finally, when they were all finished, Mr. Usher stood up slowly, pressing his hand against his back as if it hurt him to sit on the grass for so long, and brushed a few brown oak leaves off of his pants.

"*Now* we're ready to start the school year," Mr. Usher said. "Let's go to class."

When all of the students were sitting quietly at their desks, Mr. Usher went up to the long blackboard in the front of the room and took out his notepad. With a fresh piece of chalk, he copied down what was on his pad, and this is what just part of the list looked like:

People I Admire	*Why*
Amelia Earhart	Confidence
My father	Helpful
Abraham Lincoln	Vision
My cousin Benny	Happy and fun loving
My mother	Loving and caring
Martin Luther King	Stood up for what he believed
Ms. Krenna, the music teacher	Creative
My friend Penelope	Fair
My grandpa Jack	Patient

When he had finished with the entire list, Mr. Usher blew the chalk dust off of his hands and walked around to the front of the big wooden teacher's desk. He sat on the corner and looked over the top of his glasses at the Children.

"What a marvelous list of people you've made!" said Mr. Usher, smiling. "I can see exactly why you admire and respect them all. Now let me ask all of you a question. How many of you want to be like some of these people when you grow up? Do you want to be admired for the same reasons you admire these people?"

In a flash, nearly every student in the class raised his or her hand, and the few who didn't were still thinking carefully and studying the list on the board.

"Well, then," said Mr. Usher slowly, "you've just helped me decide what I'm going to teach you this year. I'm going to try to teach you to be self-confident, helpful, visionary, caring, creative, fair, courageous, patient, and all of the other things on the list. And since you all *want* to learn to be like these people, I don't imagine we'll have any arguments about our class work all year long. Any questions?"

Mr. Usher sat on the front of his big wooden desk with his arms folded and looked at the Children, and they sat at their desks and looked back at him, puzzled. Finally, Felisa threw up her arm.

"Aren't you going to teach us math and science and history and reading and writing and all of the things the other kids learn?" she asked worriedly. "How are we supposed to get smart if you don't teach us any of that?"

"Well," said Mr. Usher, with a little smile, "I *was* going to ask you if being smart and knowing a lot was something you admired, because it isn't anywhere on the list you gave me. Now that you mention it, yes, of course, I'm going to teach you math and science and history and all of the rest. Those are some of the *tools* we all need to become like the people we admire and respect. But we have to remember that knowledge is just one of our tools. If we want to grow up to be like people we admire, we have to learn much more than math and science and history."

Just about then the bell for recess rang outside the door, and the Children jumped up from their desks and began to file out the door to the playground. Mr. Usher remained seated on the front of his big desk and watched them go. As the other Children rushed out, Casey came up to Mr. Usher.

"Mr. Usher, *I* think you would have taught those things to us anyway, even if we hadn't come up with our own list," Casey said. "Am I right?"

Mr. Usher crossed his arms and smiled down at Casey. "Well," said Mr. Usher with a little chuckle, "you were all so helpful, we'll just never know, will we?" And with that, Mr. Usher gently turned Casey around and pushed him toward the door.

That recess the Children talked together and with their friends in other classes about Mr. Usher and their strange first morning of the school year. It wasn't the last time that the Children sat together under the old oak tree and talked with Mr. Usher, nor was it the last time that this new teacher surprised his students with new ideas about what were the truly important things they might learn in school.

*   *   *   *

We all have heroes. They are people who we perceive are somehow better than we are. We want to be like them. They provide for us a template of how we can feel happy and proud that we had a life on this earth. They are not perfect by any means, but they have particular characteristics that we want to combine and emulate. The great political leader may not be physically strong, and the great athlete may not be a moral visionary. The loving father may not be creative, and the faithful friend may not be an intuitive thinker. We take the pieces and ask the question, often without knowing it: how can I come closer to each of their strengths and avoid each of their weaknesses? How did each of these individuals come to personify some trait of character or being such that he or she is my hero?

Without sacrificing our concept of self, the templates of our heroes can help us know, concretely, where we want to go. Whether we admit it or not, knowing where we want to go is *always* the first step in a journey.

Step 0: Preparation

Life left untended tends to decrease options. When in doubt, the best path is always the one that increases options.
Jerry Ryan

We have all had one or two or three great teachers in our lives, either in or out of school, and we all remember and revere them amongst our personal pantheon of heroes. A great teacher can raise us to levels we never hoped to reach, just as surely as he or she can explain, in clear terms, the mysteries of calculus, the omnipotence of DNA, the overarching reach of Keats, how to hit a curve ball, or the relationship between effective employees and a good bottom line. Very simply, great teachers are *the* key to learning. We have known this in our multicultural souls since the times of Socrates, Confucius, and Jesus. No windfall of federal funding, no processional of new programs and texts, no new technology based on thin pieces of silicon will ever be as effective an educational tool as a great teacher. In this way heroes and teachers are very much the same. Our heroes and teachers, by their examples and their relationship to learning, *prepare* us to take on life's challenges.

What sets great teachers apart from good teachers and not-so-good teachers?

Truly great teachers, in the classroom, on the playing field, at home, or in business, all share one common strategy. They serve up their subject in such a way that I, the student sitting in their classroom, their locker room, or their boardroom, *feel a personal stake in learning what it is that they are trying to teach me.* I *need* to know the answers to questions that are raised. How do great teachers do that?

They do it by making us *want* to overcome the challenge of learning. Teachers who hand out a problem and say "solve it" are not great teachers, because half of the students don't give a damn about the question that was just asked. They see no reason, no compelling personal motivation to delve into the unknown to find the answer. So they don't, or they don't very well, and true learning doesn't take place. As Sizer and Sizer state in *The Students are Watching*: "Accuracy will start to matter, but only if it follows engagement, only if he (the student) has to put himself on the line."

Before we solve a problem or overcome a challenge or invent an invention or come to a personal point of realization, we have to be prepared to encounter a problem or a challenge or a quest worthy of our assault. The excitement of learning, the compelling personal drive to take one more step on the path towards wisdom, comes when we try to solve a problem we *want* to solve, when we see a challenge and say, yes, I can meet it. Great teachers lead us *just far* enough down a path so we can see a challenge for ourselves. They provide us *just enough* insight so we can work toward a solution that makes us, makes *me* want to jump up and shout out the solution to the world, makes *me* want to step to the next higher level. Great teachers somehow make us *want to ask* the questions that they want us to answer, overcome the challenge that they, because they are our teacher, believe we need to overcome.

I have never had the insight and creativity and patience of our mythical Mr. Usher. But once, fresh out of graduate school and traveling the world, I glimpsed that point where learning jumps from theory to desire. I had a job teaching college students at a university in the southern Philippines, and my students did not want to learn…

*   *   *   *

I sat on a tall lab stool looking over the rows of polite, blank, trusting faces, turned up at me, pencils gripped in eager hands. I knew they would scribe my lecture verbatim and take it as gospel. The week before I had discussed the theory of continental drift, describing the widening of the Atlantic Ocean and the lazy separation over the last 250 million years of the Euro-African and American landmasses. I joked that this inexorable shift must account for the periodic increase in phone rates between New York and London. Heads dropped and pencils squeaked as that little-known absurdity, sure to rear its trivial head on a mid-term exam, was captured in the neat pigeonholed lecture notes of almost every student. I wanted to weep.

I sat on my lab stool and gave up. For six weeks I had tried to teach the fundamentals of earth science to the freshman class at this small university in the Philippines. They were bright students, and many spoke English better than their American counterparts. But the earth is not a self-evident laboratory, sculpted in scripture or clean objectivity. The truth does not reveal itself in the techno-color simplicity of a two-hour cinema plot. Understanding takes imagination and curiosity and visualization. My students, like most, wanted to memorize my lessons, pass the test, and get on to their next class, a soccer game, or a steamy Friday night date. They did not, for the most part, give a toss about my curriculum. I couldn't blame them. Most of these students grew up in what passes for a Filipino middle class or were poor barrio children bright enough to merit one of a handful of scholarships to the school. The latest grand theories, the glossy front pages of *National Geographic* and *Scientific American*, were remote, incidental sidelines to their immediate lives. They sat through my class, politely attentive, like one might during visits with a senile grandparent.

I was formulating just the right timbre of a stern professorial rebuke when the rain hit. The classroom was on the top floor of the science building, a neat concrete, open-air structure, with wooden shutters on the windows that let in welcome evening breezes and unwelcome mosquitoes. The tropical downpour made a godly racket on the galvanized tin roof. At first far off, the thunder moved steadily closer with each successive rumble, coming from the mountains at my back. It was an evening class, and the rain poured down through the yellow wash of streetlights outside the building. The noise on the roof became deafening, and even students sitting side-by-side could not hear each other shout. They patiently doodled on their notepads.

The rain was an answered prayer. I needed to stop and think, and I hadn't any other excuse. First came a distant rushing like wind in pine trees, and then louder like muffled wheels on a fast train; a tremendous blast of air shook the shuttered windows, and the squall line hit. A sheet of lightning cut loose just over the building, searing the air with the sickly sweet smell of ozone. The students and I looked at each other helplessly.

As quickly as the squall arrived, it marched out eastward across the city and left us in quiet. As if the last thunderclap had blown the storm clear to the next island, the rain stopped, and the mosquitoes hummed back in the still, humid air.

I decided it was time for a hard change of direction. If they don't care about what I want to teach, I will teach what they care about. Maybe it will work and maybe it won't, but it couldn't be any worse than the fiasco about intercontinental telephone rates.

"Put down your pencils and close your books," I told them. "Here's your homework. For next class, each one of you will write down something that you don't understand, something that interests you that you'd like to know. Anything at all. I don't care if it's about geology or biology or politics or history, as long as it's somehow connected with the physical universe, and *you care* about the answers. Bring your questions to class. For the rest of the semester, we're going to discuss only your questions. No more textbooks and prepared lab work. No more quizzes on the last chapter. This way I'll know that at least one of you is interested in what we're discussing during our evenings together. Thank you, see you on Thursday."

On Thursday, the students sat rigidly at their desks, nervous about the untested ground in front of them. I was equally afraid of what I had promised.

I sorted the uneven stack of half-sheets of yellow and white binder paper and turned over the first page. Someone wanted to know about lightning, where it came from and what caused it. We talked about lightning and clouds and weather for a half hour, and for the first time in a month, a student asked a question. During the rainy season, it seemed easy to make weather an interesting topic. Why hadn't I thought of that?

The next scribble asked about dinosaurs, so we spent thirty minutes reliving the myths of the Jurassic, global extinctions, and the dinosaurs' halting evolution into birds. More hands were raised. Everyone loves the idea of dinosaurs, as long as we don't have to memorize long Latin names and the evolutionary order. We had a few more minutes of class time, so I turned over the next page. The question was

"Is gravity a concept or a principle?"

I read the question to the class. Blank looks. I read it to them again. More blank looks. As I looked out the window at the yellow street lights clouded with tiny insects swarming in the muggy night air, I walked back and forth in front of the chalkboard trying to gather a useful response and, failing, quietly dismissed the class.

For three days I wrestled with the question. I jotted down notes and ideas on scraps of coarse brown typing paper, and twisted them this way and that trying to come up with the answer. I thought about philosophy, physics, chemistry, and logic. I stared out my office window, past the drooping papaya trees, heavy with long orange fruit that ring the campus, and tried to ignore the mosquitoes. At night I sat in front of a waving electric fan, sweating in the still humidity, watching small pools of water condense off of cold beer bottles as if condensation might hold some insightful clue.

At the beginning of the next class, I asked who had submitted the question. No one raised a hand, which wasn't surprising since I had specifically said that the questions would be anonymous. Someone was frightened that he or she had angered the professor. I asked again, this time assuring the class that I had nothing but praise for the student who had posed this question. A young man in the back timidly raised his hand. I asked him his name and his major. He studied humanities and enjoyed literature. You have an "A" for the semester, I said. You don't have to take any exams if you don't want. You have an "A" right now because that was a marvelous, thoughtful question. Congratulations.

The other students looked at him as if he'd been suddenly ordained and won the lottery in the same day, and shouted at me for the answer.

We spent an hour discussing what we meant by the words "concept" and "principle." We discussed how different people, using different languages and with widely diverse backgrounds, form a basis of understanding that allows them to share such abstract ideas. The discussion was far more esoteric than any lecture on sedimentary processes, the fossil record, or volcanism, subjects that had put the students to sleep. They threw questions at me and at each other with the rapid enthusiasm of quiz show contestants.

We spent the next half hour discussing gravity—what it is, what are its effects, when is it a strong force, and when is it weak. We argued about why the student had cared about gravity in the first place. What relevance is there to gravity other than to keep us from falling upwards into outer space? We talked about gravity as a metaphor for entire portfolios of scientific postulates, and the students kept firing questions and answers.

Finally I explained my answer as simply as I could, reducing three days of internal angst to a few sentences, a concise proof. They held their breaths and hung on every word. No one wrote a single note. I didn't hear mosquitoes humming or children kicking the soccer ball on the dimly lit playing fields outside the classroom. For the first time in half a semester, the students and I shared a reverence for the quest of understanding. They just wanted to know my answer because it had become important to them. I nearly wept, but this time with the joy and relief that I later felt when my children were born.

Over the next three months, we waded through their stack of questions, and occasionally I slipped in a few of my own, largely so I could pretend to complete a class in earth science. Rarely did a night go by without a heated argument about one or more of our topics. The questions became more and more sophisticated as each student reached to duplicate that magic automatic "A" that had fallen like manna from heaven. Regardless of their motives, the students pushed themselves to learn something new every hour of every class. In the end, we'd covered most of the major points of my original syllabus, though neither the students nor I would be able to reconstruct just how or in what order. The final exam was a masterpiece but can never be used again.

Oh, the answer to the question. Is gravity a concept or a principle? Over the years, I've thought and rethought the question and have occasionally changed my answer. Sometimes I come back to the original conclusion, and then I change my mind again. My answer is not important. Yours is.

$$*\qquad*\qquad*\qquad*$$

Great teachers create opportunities for students to ask questions that excite them to self-discovery. Great leaders, in business, politics, sports, or families, create opportunities for others to be self-successful. Many of our heroes are heroes because they find a way for us to find something within ourselves—courage, kindness, leadership, charity, vision—that we might not have found without their help. They prepare us to be prepared to take advantage of opportunities.

The first task of preparation is to create or take advantage of, the opportunity to explore, learn, lead, or challenge.

*   *   *   *

The Lesson of Sunny

Often after school let out, on a mild spring day, or when the autumn winds stirred up brown leaves on the baring forest trees, Mr. Usher would walk through the forest that grew close in to the little town in the valley. As he strolled through the shady glens and sunny meadows, he sometimes met up with an old man who lived deep in the forest in a small house by himself. The old man had moved to our valley many years ago from the faraway lands of China. His name when he lived in China was Sun Tzu, but because of his friendly smile and warm hospitality, Mr. Usher called him Sunny for short. (Remember, just as Mr. Sun is *our* guide, Sunny is a guide to Mr. Usher. In the end, we will find that even teachers need teachers sometimes.) Sunny walked with his back bent over, a cane of smooth wood grasped firmly in one hand. Each day he gathered especially delicious mushrooms and herbs in the forest and sold them in the farmer's market on market day. Mr. Usher said that Sunny was as old as the forest, though he still could walk as far in a day as Mr. Usher himself.

Sometimes when Mr. Usher met Sunny in the woods, and after Sunny's bag was full of herbs and mushrooms and maybe some wild berries when they were in season, the two men would go back to Sunny's old house deep in the forest, and sit on the porch and drink tea. Then, with a handshake, and knowing that they would meet again soon, Mr. Usher would walk back through the forest to the schoolyard and home.

On this particular day, Mr. Usher found Sunny collecting herbs near to his house, and the first thing that Mr. Usher noticed was that Sunny was not smiling. This was most unusual, and Mr. Usher was concerned, but for a while the two friends worked quietly side-by-side filling Sunny's basket. Then when the basket was full and they were both sitting comfortably on the shady porch, with a fresh pot of tea between them, Mr. Usher asked the old man what was bothering him.

"Many, many years ago, longer ago than you might think, when I was still a young man living in the mountains and forests of China, I wrote a short book, a very short book, really, no more than a few hundred lines. As a child

I had watched and learned from the land around me. I lived for some years in a monastery where the monks spent their days thinking about the customs of man and nature. And later, I lived in the great home of a nobleman, and was an apprentice to his chief falconer, because I knew the ways of the forest and of the hunt. I passed many afternoons training the birds and learning how and when to hunt for prey, and how and when to stay at home. Of course sometimes our warriors went off to fight, because in those days the noblemen who ruled our land always seemed to squabble about one thing or another. When the warriors came back home, I would listen to them, and I learned quite a bit about the ways of battle.

"Over time I set down on paper my thoughts about how we find our way through life. It was clear to me that whether one is learning about the forest, or training falcons, or hunting in the mountains, or meditating in the temple, or fighting a battle, the strategies to be successful at all of these tasks are very much the same. So I wrote down my ideas, and it was a very short book indeed."

Sunny stopped to sip his tea and look off into the distance as if he were seeing his mountain home in his faraway land.

"This sounds like something to be proud of," said Mr. Usher. "Why then are you not smiling when you tell this story?"

"Even living this far in the forest, I hear news. I've heard that somehow many people have read my small book, and in fact some of these other people have written books of their own about the meaning of *my* book. Of course, I'm flattered that they should take the time, but I think that there are parts that they don't understand.

"I wrote the book in the language of war, as if all challenges we face in life were a battle and the strategies we use to overcome challenges, to create new opportunities, and to solve problems were the strategies that a general or a great warrior might use to achieve victory over his enemy. So the people who read my book at first thought I was a warrior, and that the book was about how to fight wars.

"Then, others read my book and thought that the ideas were about how to run a successful business. They think that doing business is a lot like battle, except no one gets killed. I guess some of the ideas in my book can help to make one wealthy and help to make one's business thrive. I must admit that all of these people are right, but it makes me sad that most people think that I'm only concerned about killing and winning and beating another person at business. It's not really what the book is about at all."

Mr. Usher wrinkled his brow in heavy thought, and the cup of tea grew cold in his hand. The old friend next to him slumped over more than usual in his chair, and for the first time, the old man looked truly old.

"Perhaps I can understand the problem better if I read your book, Sunny," said Mr. Usher hopefully. "Do you have a copy here? If it's as short as you say, I'd like to read it and then we can talk about it."

"Yes, yes, I have an old copy here somewhere, though I imagine you can't read the original in Chinese," Sunny said, with a hint of a twinkle in his eye. "I'll have to let you read the translated version." And with that, Sunny pulled himself out of the deep chair on the porch and shuffled slowly into the house. After a few minutes, he came out again with a fresh pot of tea and an old thin book, bound in worn leather, which he handed over to Mr. Usher.

"Make yourself at home," Sunny said. "I'm going to take a nap. If you want to talk about the book later, we can." And with that, Sunny lay down in a heavy canvas hammock that stretched between two poles on the porch and shut his eyes, and Mr. Usher took up the book and settled down to read.

Sunny woke from his nap when a cool breeze swept over the porch, tingling the few green leaves that had sprouted on the live oaks and cottonwoods that surrounded his little house. Mr. Usher sat in the same chair on the porch with the thin book in his lap and stared thoughtfully out through the trees. He turned as Sunny slowly climbed out of the hammock and sat down again in his chair.

"I can see why your readers believe this book is about war and conflict," said Mr. Usher. "Every line talks about battles and generals, warriors and spies, killing and setting fires. It does indeed seem like a cookbook for how to beat an enemy."

"You are absolutely right," said Sunny with a little smile crossing his deeply cracked face. "But only in the case of war should that enemy be an army.

"Here is what I believe. The great panorama of life contains, for each of us, an endless series of challenges, problems, and opportunities. Some are small, some large, some that are but a mild nuisance or a chance to brighten one day, and others that can change our entire life, for better or for worse. Happiness and success depend, in many ways, on one's ability to calmly overcome challenges, to successfully solve problems, and to creatively take advantage of opportunities. If we let these problems and challenges push us around, dictate to us where we are going in life, then we are usually not happy. If we take control of our lives, using the skills and wisdom that we learn as we grow up, then we usually are happy. It's as simple as that. In short, except for a lucky few, *happiness doesn't just happen.*

"I chose the language of war for my little book because battle is all too common, and many people, especially in the old days, understood this language. Some of what I wrote is specific to winning in war, because war is one type of problem. But see here. Replace some of the words I have used in my book, and see how the meaning then reaches far beyond the task of the general or king or warrior or business executive who is trying to defeat his competition.

"Each of us may be a *warrior*, a *general*, or a *nation*. Warriors and generals are people who understand how to use their resources to achieve their goals. They may be parents, teachers, business leaders, mediators, coaches, falconers, students, anyone.

"The *enemy or opponent* is any challenge, problem, or opportunity to be studied, met, analyzed, and solved.

"*Battles, military operations, and armed struggles* are the process of seeking solutions, overcoming challenges, and creating new ways in which to find the success and happiness we seek.

"*The land, the terrain, the earth*, the very contours of the hills and the nature of the ground are the aspects, the characteristics, the constitution of the problems that we face.

"*Armies, soldiers, and spies*, like knowledge itself, are the tools and skills we each have and use to meet the challenges and solve the problems we encounter.

"*Victory* means finding a solution, a way through the obstacles, overcoming a challenge, the taking of one more unobstructed step down the path towards the life we each desire.

"These are the keys to strategy."

Mr. Usher listened intently as Sunny spoke, as closely as his own students listened when Mr. Usher asked them to gather 'round the front of the room for something important. Mr. Usher only wished he had his big pad of paper or his chalkboard so he could copy down what Sunny said to remember it better.

"I think I understand," said Mr. Usher slowly. "But it would really help me if you could give me an example. It still seems to me that your book is more about war than it is about solving problems."

"Gladly," said Sunny.

"Well, for example," said Mr. Usher, opening the book without looking and picking out a passage to read, "here you say 'The good fighters of old first put themselves beyond the possibility of defeat, and then waited for an opportunity of defeating the enemy.' What does that mean if it doesn't have to do with war and warriors?"

"It's very clear," began Sunny, looking more like a professor in front of a class than an old, stooped herb collector. "This means that if you want to be successful at meeting life's challenges, you must first prepare your own skills. The skills are many: vision, patience, understanding, discrimination, clarity, confidence, and so forth. Then when a problem or challenge presents itself, you will be ready and able to create solutions. Preparation in advance of facing problems is the key to overcoming them. What is disappointing is that after so many years we still refuse to overtly teach these most prized skills to our young people."

"And here," asked Mr. Usher, "what does it mean when you say 'Numerical weakness comes from having to prepare against possible attacks; numerical strength, from compelling our adversary to make these preparations against us'? I would think having more troops than your opponent does is always an advantage."

"Remember, you must think not in terms of war but in terms of your personal strengths and tools. This means that power and numerical superiority do not mean anything, because most problems do not involve physical conflict. Power and numbers can even provide a false sense of security, so you do not fully understand the challenges that you face. It is not the quantity of the troops that you have, but the depth of your skills and your personal resources, and how well you are prepared to use these skills that will determine your success."

"And what about this one?" asked Mr. Usher. "You write 'Rapidity is the essence of war: take advantage of the enemy's unreadiness, make your way by unexpected routes, and attack unguarded spots.' That certainly sounds like a strategy for attacking and winning a battle to me."

"Remember who we are talking about," said Sunny patiently. "This means that we need to be creative in coming up with ideas and solutions to the challenges and problems that we face. Solutions are often found by testing many different assumptions and ideas to see what works, creating options that look at the problem in new ways. Problems have weaknesses, just like people. Exploiting the weakness of a problem is the surest path to a solution. Stay ahead of the problem; don't let it overwhelm you, just as you would stay ahead of an army that was chasing you down from the side or from the rear."

Mr. Usher thought about what Sunny had said for a long time. Sunny sat calmly and watched as the sun fell below the trees in front of the cabin. Small flocks of blackbirds settled noisily in the live oak trees, squawking and ruffling their wings before settling down to the even dusk. Finally, Mr. Usher turned back to Sunny, and the old man was smiling as he used to when they picked mushrooms together in the forest.

"I spend my whole life with the Children," said Mr., Usher, "trying to teach them how to ask questions and solve problems and think for themselves. You've thought about these same things for a long time, and your book has many lessons to teach me. If you don't mind, I'd like to reread your book now that I understand the main points that you were trying to make, and then I'm sure I'll have more questions."

"By all means," said Sunny. "Why don't you spend the night here with me, and we can talk all you want. It's been a long time since I spoke about these ideas and I miss it. I used to spend days on end, watching my falcons fly across the meadows, thinking of each bird as a tool that I alone could direct against some challenge or problem in my life. We worked so well together, my birds and I, that sometimes it seemed that we could do anything together. Talking with you will help me to remember those days and ideas from long ago."

So the two men gathered up food from the kitchen to make their supper, and Mr. Usher carried in several armloads of dry oak and cedar so they would have a roaring fire against the cold night air. After dinner, with the dishes washed and set upon the rack to dry by the sink, and with a healthy fire crackling in the fireplace, the friends drew their chairs up to the hearth and talked late into the night, poring over the thin book and picking apart the ideas of each passage. Finally the old man grew sleepy and begged to be allowed to go to bed. Even though Mr. Usher would have liked to talk all night about Sunny's ideas, they each went off to bed though Mr. Usher spent a long time looking out the window of the small guest room.

In the morning, Mr. Usher woke and walked out to the porch to find Sunny, hand open and full of seeds, covered in birds as he stood quietly and let them feed. When his hand was nearly empty, he tossed the last few seeds up into the air, and the birds rose up around him and flew off, twittering, into the forest. The old man sat down in his chair in the sun and pulled an old blanket onto his lap.

"I don't think I'll go out into the forest today," said Sunny. "It seems a good day to sit in the sun and watch the world go by."

"Last night I couldn't go to sleep after our long talk, so I got up and wrote down some of the things we talked about. I hope that's all right," said Mr. Usher.

"Of course it's all right, my friend," said Sunny. "They are just words and they can live on a page as well as in the air or in one's mouth. As a matter of fact, ever since I heard that all of these books have been written about *my* book, I've been meaning to write some clarifications down myself, just so people understand that war wasn't what I was writing about all those years ago. Do you think that's a good idea?"

Mr. Usher jumped up off the porch railing where he had been perched. "I think it's a wonderful idea!" he exclaimed. "I know that your eyes are not as good as they used to be, and your hand not as steady. If I can help to write down your thoughts, I would be more than happy to help."

So the two friends decided that day that they would meet from time to time and go over Sunny's book carefully and thoughtfully and add some thoughts and clarifications where they might. They worked that day, and all of the next, and every few days, or on the weekend, for half a year, Mr. Usher went out into the forest to meet with the old man until finally they were finished. Ever since then, Mr. Usher has used many of Sunny's ideas when he is teaching the Children, and he never stops wondering that so many of the ideas are helpful to the Children, young and old.

*   *   *   *

We turn around to find ancient Mr. Sun, who of course is laughing at our confusion. He has just watched with us as his much younger-looking reflection Sunny has led Mr. Usher through a discussion of their book's meaning. Well, we all have our own teachers, and for good reason in the end. But for now, a little confusion is not the end of the world.

Mr. Sun is looking over the rice paper manuscript again.

"And by the way, some of what I wrote in *The Art of War* having to do with fire and sieges … well some of it *is* about war and nothing else. Don't be confused. I had to make a living as a consultant, and the ancient warlords needed to win battles! But back to the business of preparation. Unless we are prepared to start the journey, it is doubtful that we will succeed in getting anywhere. And as we will see later, there are times when we don't have the luxury of patient thought and analysis. We need to know something about the process before we need to use it. If a cook has not learned how to boil water, he will not be successful when called upon to cook a ten-course meal for the emperor."

We have busily written down Mr. Sun's comments and now refer to his manuscript to find examples that deal specifically with the importance of preparation.

We select passages that we find in his manuscript that seem to address the role of preparation, using the definitions we have selected.

Sun Tzu writes: *Whoever is first in the field and awaits the coming of the enemy, will be fresh for the fight; whoever is second in the field and has to hasten to battle will arrive exhausted.*

This means that vision, the ability to forecast and look ahead, is a key to preparedness. If you know that problems and challenges are a part of life, that they always lie ahead, and you are ready to meet them, you will be prepared when they arrive. We can view the process of solving problems and overcoming challenges as a battle if we view the challenge or problem itself as our opponent. Successful companies use strategic planning tools to look into the future, to forecast both opportunities for growth and pitfalls that may threaten their success. Successful organizations and individuals remember the simple tenets of Murphy's Law: *that which can go wrong will go wrong.* Preparing in advance may be as simple as practicing a fire drill or adding to a savings account or as subtle as practicing equanimity in the face of chaos.

Sun Tzu writes: *Thus it is that in war the victorious strategist only seeks battle after the victory has been won, whereas he who is destined to defeat first fights and afterwards looks for victory.*

This means that with preparation and confidence, you will overcome the challenges in your path. With a good strategy and good understanding of the personal and external resources available to you, you will succeed. Without these, you will ultimately fail, despite your best intentions. Two experienced business partners know that a well-crafted contract *before* they begin to work will save the cost of disagreement later on. Do they write a contract expecting to fight over the terms of the agreement? No. They discuss the nature of their relationship and put it on paper in order to minimize disagreements *before* they occur. How similar is the successful marriage, where two people get to know each other in advance of their vows, winning through communication that which might later be lost through conflict?

Sun Tzu writes: *Though according to our estimate the soldiers of the enemy exceed our own in number, that shall advantage them nothing in the matter of victory. I say that victory can still be achieved.*

This means that power and numbers are not necessarily keys to solving problems. These may even provide a false sense of security. Napoleon amassed an army so large that it could not be defeated on the field of battle by the Russians. The French army could not, however, defeat the Russian winter and the length of its own supply lines, and, in part due to its sheer mass, failed. The key to success lay not with numbers, but with strategy that took into account far more variables than the size and experience of the opposing armies.

Sun Tzu writes: *The art of war teaches us to rely not on the likelihood of the enemy's not coming, but on our own readiness to receive him; not on the chance of his not attacking, but rather on the fact that we have made our position unassailable.*

This means that problems inevitably arise. They are a part of life. Without them life would be dull and static. If we look forward to challenges and seek out opportunities for growth, we will hone our skills to the point that even the more difficult problems will not overwhelm us. To a child every problem is cause for anxiety; he or she does not have the experience to keep small problems in perspective. With experience, we learn to manage life's hurdles, to see how some of them can lead to opportunities. We welcome the boss who asks us to shoulder additional responsibilities as this leads to personal and professional growth. As our confidence and ability to deal with problems and opponents grow, we ask the coach to give us the ball and let us lead the team because we know that our preparation gives the team the best chance of winning.

We ask Mr. Sun if we have correctly interpreted his meaning, given the definitions he provided. He says, yes, in this context we are close, though he is sure that additional meditation on the points will give us a fuller understanding yet. He hopes that we recognize the importance he has placed on preparation.

We conclude that *a clear sense of the strengths and weaknesses of the resources at our command is the second task of preparation.*

Mr. Sun sneaks a long piece of chalk out of the arm of his gown and approaches a small blackboard that has suddenly appeared at his side. He holds his hands behind his back professorially.

"There is one more aspect of preparation that is critical, that is usually assumed, and we all know that assumption is an extremely dangerous proposition. It is usually assumed because, by definition, if you and I are talking, or our reader is reading, then we share a certain level of communication. Were I to switch to my native tongue (and Mr. Sun does so, speaking an ancient dialect from the west of Hunan, which is of course impossible for us to understand) you and I could not communicate at all.

"But there are many more subtle barriers to communication as well, and if we cannot, or do not chose to overcome these barriers, we will encounter life decisions and try to solve problems and do a lot of falconing all by ourselves with little, if any, success. Even in the briefest of communications, people develop and share common models that allow them to communicate effectively. If you don't share the model, you can't communicate. If you can't communicate, you can't teach, learn, lead, or follow.

"Some of our strongest ideas are couched in terms that others will not or cannot understand. Questions of personal or social morality, shared vision, community consciousness, ethics, philosophy, spirituality, hope, fear: all of these contain subjective elements that require a shared understanding, a shared vocabulary. Without this shared perspective, how do we argue with and learn from our teachers and classmates, our parents and bosses and employees?

"So how do we find common models?" It seems to us that Mr. Sun's question is rhetorical, so we keep our thoughts to ourselves and listen.

"Logic is one answer. The rules of logic are universal, which is why mathematicians and logicians from different cultures and backgrounds can converse. It's very easy to agree on terms of logic."

Mr. Sun turns to his blackboard and writes in large block letters:

If A, then B.
A is true.
Then B must be true.

"This is the simplest logical statement of all," he explains. "If *A* happens, then *B* will follow. *A* does, in fact, happen. The result is *B*. It doesn't matter in the least what *A* and *B* are; if one believes in the most elementary kind of logic, this result is absolutely inevitable. If two people can't agree that this sequence of statements is correct, they will never be able to communicate. Two people may have a hard time agreeing on a wide range of subjective ideas, but may still fall back on objective logic to communicate functionally.

"Beyond logic and mathematics, though, just about every other form of communication is fraught with pitfalls. Therefore we first investigate common and uncommon ground. Israelis and Palestinians have a hard time finding common ground. Both want peace and stability and good things for their children, but they have fundamentally different views of the world, and on how to obtain the stability and peace that they seek. Parents and children often have a hard time finding common ground. They share a home and love and dreams of the future, but their language and self-perceptions are often dramatically out of synch. Owners and employees, Democrats and Republicans, teachers and students, Shiites and Sunnis, men and women, blacks, whites, Asians, Hispanics … without an understanding of our mutual frames of reference, effective communication is difficult. Despite our best wishes, we are *not* all on the same page.

"Using common models of communication is important because it simplifies the complex. Two girlfriends try to decide what to wear to school tomorrow. Do they spend hours analyzing and defining why a particular choice of clothing is aesthetically pleasing from the point of view of color coordination, style, fabric, and cost. No. More likely, they say the clothes are either 'cool' or 'not cool,' and the discussion is done. They have achieved their objective, they both understand the result, and therefore the question has been answered to their mutual satisfaction.

"So right here, at the beginning, you and I and our reader have a real problem, one that we have to solve on faith for the moment. None of us know much at all about each other, so we cannot assume a common framework for communication, just as a teacher at the beginning of the school year knows little about each of his students. At the beginning, then, we might all be a bit confused. That's okay. The goal is to understand more at the end than we did at the start, so for now, let's plunge ahead and see if we come up with shared understanding."

It sounds straight forward to us, particularly if we can always fall back on the tests of simple logic to see if we are being led astray. Mr. Sun has not asked us to make any leaps of faith yet, just that we be patient.

We conclude that the third critical task of preparation is to find a shared basis upon which to communicate.

Mr. Sun tells us to put away the rice paper and get on with our work.

When we have a personal, inexorable stake in our quest, when we know our own skills, and when we can share our visions, plans, creations, and knowledge with others, we are prepared to begin.

What's next?

Step 1: The Art of Questioning

Questions are how you develop strategy.
Michael Moreno, Falconer Class of 1999

The difference between grappling and other forms of learning is that when the questions become the students' own, so do the answers.
Sizer and Sizer, *The Students are Watching*

Our educational systems have been constructed entirely around the goal of providing the correct answer to a question provided by an instructor or handed out on a standardized exam. This system provides a form of valid comparison for the results of a group of students, and it provides a foundation of shared information amongst those who have followed a course of study. Unfortunately, the real world, particularly the real world of the coming century, does not and will not work this way. Our heroes are not defined by how well they answered canned questions or what they scored on their SATs precisely because these outcomes do not determine success in real-world situations. The real revolution in education and training, if it comes, will be overtly switching our priority from the skills of giving answers to the skills of finding new questions.

Questions are waypoints on the path of wisdom. Each question leads to one or more new questions or answers. Sometimes *answers* are dead ends; they don't lead anywhere. *Questions* are never dead ends. Every question has the inherent potential to lead to a new level of discovery, understanding, or creation, levels that can range from the trivial to the sublime.

In our Falconer seminar, we relied on the time-tested methods of Socrates to stimulate discussion based on the students' personal passions and ability to create lines of inquiry. How? With computer programs? With Internet searches? No. We simply asked one question after another. The one requirement I had for the course was that at any time on any day I might ask any student "What do you want to talk about today?" and they had to be ready with a question for the group to pursue.

We all spend way too much time trying to find answers when questions are vastly more important. So where do questions come from? Where better to look than in the classroom.

*   *   *   *

The Lesson of Questions

Early autumn in the valley is always a time of fresh cool breezes, clean air, field grasses growing bent and brown, and wood smoke smells in the afternoon. A few weeks before Halloween the farmers bring their pumpkins and late harvest into town, the sky grows dark each day by supper time, and the students have settled down from the lazy summer vacations to another year of learning.

One day in their first year with Mr. Usher, a month or so after the start of the school year, the Children arrived in the morning to find their classroom turned, well, upside down.

Not upside down actually, maybe more inside out. As the Children entered through the door and took off their coats and caps, they found their desks rearranged so that Mr. Usher's big wooden desk, rather than set at its normal spot in front of the class under the blackboard, was set at the back of the room, facing all of the student desks, lined up closely in front. Mr. Usher sat at his big desk, facing forward, his hands folded quietly in front of him. He motioned for the Children to find their seats, which took a few minutes because none of the seats were in their right places at all.

When the Children were are all seated and quiet, Mr. Usher began.

"We haven't known each other all that long, but we have been in class now for several weeks, and it is time for some tests."

The Children groaned.

Mr. Usher drew down the corners of his mouth in mock sadness. "What, you don't like tests?" he asked. "I thought all students *loved* tests. Maybe you just have never taken *my* kind of test, so give me a chance to explain.

"There is a reason I changed the desks around today. We have covered a lot of material in science, English, and ancient history so far, and you are going to create the tests in these subjects. And if you do a good job, which I know you will, you can write all the tests all year long."

Now you will remember that the Children were pretty surprised that first day of school when Mr. Usher took them to sit under the big oak tree and they talked about heroes and all. But you should have seen the looks on the Children's faces when their teacher told them that *they* got to write the tests in his class! The Children were shouting and high-fiving and dreaming of straight-A report cards as Mr. Usher tried to quiet them down.

"I'm glad you are so enthusiastic about this," he said, "though I'm a little bit surprised. Coming up with questions for a test is a *lot* harder than coming up with the answers, you know."

"What do you mean?" asked Teresa, still a big smile on her face. "We can ask any questions we want. How hard is that?"

"We'll see," said Mr. Usher. "First, I need someone to write our questions down on the board. You all pretend you are the teachers and I am the student. Let's start with our science test for the last unit we studied."

So one at a time and then in a flood, the Children shouted out questions for the test on a science unit about evaporation. Soon they had a long list of questions on the board:

What are the three states of water?
How does water evaporate?
What happens when water vapor comes into contact with a cold surface?
What two elements make up a water molecule?
Why does water evaporate?
Where in nature do we see examples of evaporation?

And lots more.

Mr. Usher nodded thoughtfully with a small smile on his face. "Those are all very good questions, and you have proven my point exactly. Since I am the student who has to answer these questions, I *know* I'll get an A on the test. All I have to do is read the book. All of the answers to these questions are right there! How easy is that?"

The Children all had puzzled looks on their faces.

"Well, of course, it would be easy for you; you're a teacher," Teresa said. "We're just students and haven't learned all of this yet."

Mr. Usher pursed his lips thoughtfully. "Sure you have. Is there anyone in this room who can't find the answer to these questions in the science book?"

The Children all looked at each other, a few thumbed their science books nervously, and then they all nodded "yes," they could find the answers to that set of questions without a problem.

"Well, personally," said Mr. Usher, "I would be pretty annoyed at wasting my time finding answers to a bunch of questions that someone else had already answered. Where is the fun in that? To my way of thinking, there is a reason we call these things 'tests.' In addition to meaning 'examination,' the word test can also mean 'to challenge' or 'to push,' and you are not pushing or challenging me a bit with questions with such easy answers. I know you can do better than that."

Since there was nothing but blank looks on the Children's faces, Mr. Usher went on. "Look at the first word in each question you have listed. All of the questions start with

Who
What
Where
When
Why
How

"These are very good words with which to start a question. The problem is that, for the most part, each question has a single answer. Question, answer, done. And since we know that the answers are all in the book already, you don't have to *think* in the process; all you have to do is *remember*. The exception is the word 'why'. 'Why' is a better way to start a question because there may be more than one reason something happens. But even the 'Why' questions we have listed can all be pretty well answered by looking in the book and seeing what someone else has decided is true."

"There are two little words that are the best question words I know. Let's try them out. Let's come up with some questions for the science test that start with the words:

What if?

"Go back to the list of questions on the board, and see if you can turn them into more challenging or interesting questions by starting with 'what if.'"

The Children all looked up at the board and scratched their heads and thought for a few minutes. Finally, Michael raised his hand.

"What if water did not evaporate?" he asked. "That would be pretty interesting, wouldn't it? I mean the whole world would be a very different place if water did not evaporate. It would be fun to think about, and the answer isn't in the book."

"What if water evaporated at really cool temperatures instead of at warm temperatures?" asked Casey. "There might be a lot more ice at the poles and maybe a lot less water in the oceans."

"What if water molecules were made up of four atoms instead of three atoms?" asked Andy. "Maybe they would be too heavy to evaporate at all!"

Suddenly many of the Children were coming up with "what if" questions as fast as they could be written down on the blackboard. But then Dana, who had been sitting quietly through all of the question-listing, stood up and raised her arms in the air.

"Hold on a minute," Dana said sternly. "You are all asking questions about how the world would be if it were different, but the world *isn't* different.

It's the way it is. Water *does* evaporate, and water *is* made up of three atoms, not four. I want to answer questions that have a single real answer in the real world. Why are we asking questions that aren't aimed at getting to real answers?"

Mr. Usher smiled his broad smile, pushed back from this desk at the back of the class, and walked up to the blackboard.

"Dana asks an excellent question," began Mr. Usher, "and it goes straight to the heart of why questions are so important. In fact, questions, and how we create them, are *far* more important than answers. Let's diagram a path of questions out on the board and see where the process leads.

"Let's draw a circle on the board to symbolize the start of the questioning process. The circle represents what we know at an instant in time, before we ask any questions. Let's call this point A.

"For example, let's say this point A represents what we know about evaporation today. Now let's ask a question from the first list on the board. Let's use the question 'Why does water evaporate?' and represent that question with an arrow."

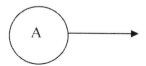

"Now we go to our books or ask our teacher, or go to the library and find the answer. We now have a new set of knowledge that we can represent by a circle we can call point B.

"The knowledge at point B is that water evaporates because heat added to the water gives the molecules more energy, and eventually they enter into a gaseous state. Let's now follow this knowledge with another question: 'Where does the heat come from?' Again we can look for the answer and represent this with another arrow and a new point C that contains the information that most energy to evaporate water comes directly or indirectly from the sun.

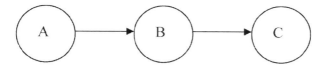

"I imagine at this point," said Mr. Usher, "that Dana is relatively happy. We have asked a series of questions, found the answers, and are more knowledgeable than we were when we started. Is that correct?"

Dana nodded her head, indicating that she was satisfied.

"Now let's see what would happen if we start back at point A with the same amount of knowledge but ask one or more 'what if' questions." Mr. Usher drew the first circle with a large *A* in the middle.

"We start by knowing what we have learned about evaporation, and ask the question 'what if water evaporated at a much lower temperature?' There is not one possible answer, but many possible answers to this question, so our diagram would have to look like this:

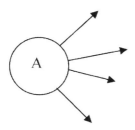

"Each arrow represents a possible direction this question can take us in seeking knowledge about the nature of evaporation. How much ice would be at the poles? How much water in the oceans? What would happen to weather patterns and rainfall and crops? How would this impact the temperature on the surface of the earth, and how would that in turn impact evaporation even further?

"For each arrow we then go to our books, our teachers, the library, and our other resources and look for answers. Since some of these questions are quite theoretical, there will not be a single answer; we will have to think about what we know and what we don't know, and probably ask some more questions. I think you can see how, pretty quickly, our diagram is going to look like this:

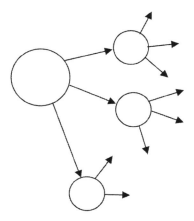

"Remember, we started each set of questions with the same amount of initial knowledge. But by asking a single 'what if' question, look how much more we have challenged ourselves. With all this thought and analysis and information gathering, just think how much more knowledge we end up with. Now that's what I would call a 'test' worthy of our class."

Dana raised her hand.

"That still does not answer my question. Why do we care about how the world *might be* instead of how it *is*? I think all of these questions are a waste of time when there is so much *real* stuff to learn. If we follow all of those arrows, we are going to end up with a huge amount of information about only one subject, and not have time to ask and answer any other questions. How do we learn about all the things we need to really know?"

"That is an excellent point," said Mr. Usher. "We have to decide why we are asking questions in the first place. Is it to get a quick answer, and then to move on to another question? If our main goal is to gain *knowledge*, then that is what we are likely to do. Or is it to delve deeply into the nature of something that makes us curious in order to push the boundaries of our understanding? If our goal is *wisdom*, then the process of creating questions and seeking answers may be more important than the answers themselves. We need to know this at the beginning, or we risk wasting a lot of time, one way or the other.

"Both methods of asking questions have a role in our lives. In most of your classes, though, you are 'tested' by the method that Dana prefers. You are asked to replay an answer that has already been found. That's why in my class we are going to test ourselves with answers that have not been found. There are times in your lives that you will need or want to make quick work of a question; there will be other times when you might want to spend weeks or months or a lifetime pondering and prodding a question as deeply and creatively as possible. We need practice at both."

And so the Children spent the rest of the day creating a test for Mr. Usher to take on the subject of evaporation. They poked and prodded the subject as best they could, and in the end came up with some very creative questions indeed. Of course by the time it came to actually take the test, they had all looked at the issue of evaporation from so many different angles and had thought so much about the subject that most of them wrote answers to the test worthy of a true scientist. Each week or so, for the rest of that year, the Children would get together to write the tests on history or English or art or whatever they had been studying, and each time they got better and better at asking questions that truly made them understand the nature of their studies.

Some of the students who, like Dana, preferred their questions cut and dried with one answer, were no doubt frustrated. They felt constantly on the perimeter of complete understanding but never at the center of it. Mr. Usher took these students aside from time to time and reassured them that, in life, being wrong a thousand times is sometimes better than being right once.

*   *   *   *

As we watch the Children finish one of their self-written tests and rush out of doors to play on the grass, we find ourselves catapulted into a cavernous, musty reading room, full of heavy, old walnut tables beneath a vaulted ceiling of flying buttresses and stained glass. A rhomboid splash of golden sunlight spotlights terrazzo mosaics on the well-worn stone floor. Stacks of leather-bound books recede like fortress walls into the dimly lit reaches of this yawning repository. Somewhere in the distance, a hollow-toned clock beats the cadence of time.

Mr. Sun sits across the table while finishing this lesson on Mr. Usher and the Children and their tests along with us. Since there does not seem to be anyone else in this enormous library who might be bothered by a bit of quiet conversation, we ask Mr. Sun if he would be so kind as to give us his view of the bit we have just read.

"I would be happy to," Mr. Sun answers, tipping back in his chair in an informal way that would surprise us if we actually expected a librarian to walk by.

"Answers are overrated. The most that an answer can offer is the temporary end to a single line of important questions. Questions, however, can lead to *many* new points of information. Questions are the source of inquiry and creativity. They multiply the diversity and scope of the learning process. Look around you at these books. Most of them were written in order to answer a question, and many of them succeeded. That leaves a lot fewer unanswered questions in the world! In fact, since most of us aren't creative geniuses, most of the answers we are likely to seek have already been found. We just need to come to a place like this, look long enough, and we will probably find that someone else has done our work for us. What fun is that? Hardly work worthy of a warrior." Mr. Sun sniffs as if offended by the direction of the issue.

"Here is an example. In my time we did not have such a thing as lawyers, but you do now. You don't *really* hate lawyers as people, but you often make jokes about them and show disdain for what they represent. The reason is that your lawyers are two-dimensional beings in a three dimensional world. They are paid to argue black against white, when we all know that shades of gray contain most of the fabric of our lives. If a question can only be argued from one side or the other, and nowhere in between, it is hardly worthy of our attention. Almost nothing in the world is that simple, and if it is, there will be little new ground to discover. When we take the time to be creative, to explore, to get out in front of the world around us, we don't want to allow over-simplicity to destroy the realm of possible discovery. We want to plow new ground.

"How do we know if we are getting the most out of our ability to ask good questions? The best test of any question is to argue both sides with equal conviction. Find a good question. Take the side you like the best, make your arguments, and then play devil's advocate against yourself. Argue against your own best arguments. All the easy, and probably unsatisfactory, potential solutions fall right away; what remains is an intelligent path to look for better ones.

"Questions often hide from us, like insects under a pile of stones. We have to turn over the stones to find them. What we see may not be pretty and well organized, it may interfere with the way we want the world to be, and we may have to paw through muck. But that's where the question lies, and without questions, we will never begin the path of discovery."

Mr. Sun bids us a happy and productive afternoon, pushes his chair away from the table, and walks off through the stacks of books, seeming to disappear more quickly than one would think possible, but maybe it is just a trick of the shafts of sunlight and their swirling motes.

*   *   *   *

The Importance of Questioning Authority

When I was young, my parents used a term that may no longer be in the American mainstream lexicon. Actually it was a father term; I can't remember anyone's mother calling her child a "wiseacre" when they talked back or smarted off in saucy juvenile superiority. Now we call someone a smartass, which means the same thing, but sounds tougher and more vulgar.

When questioning authority, there is a very fine line between being a wiseacre and a revolutionary. Both say what the authority does not want to hear. Success depends as much on how it is said as on what is said. In the revolutionary 1960s, we had posters and lapel pins that shouted, simply "Question Authority." I swore I would allow my children to wear those when they came of questioning age.

Many centuries before those turbulent 1960s, the *Tao* spoke of rivers and stones. If you sit by the rapids of a white water stream, you see the water pounding against the obstructing rocks, solid matter preventing the rushing liquid from seeking its inevitable way downhill. The *Tao* teaches us that the rocks are wasting their time. Over the millennia, the water will wear the rock away. But step back and look at this relationship from the point of view of the entire river: the vast majority of the water in the river is not hitting against the rocks at all. The water finds alternate paths, where the obstructions are fewer, finding a way downhill around the obstacles, not through them. Water spends far less energy running downhill unobstructed than it does eroding rocks.

Both the revolutionary and the wiseacre need to decide their objective. Is change most important, or is the mechanism of demanding change most important? Authority is, by definition, a potential obstruction to change, whether it is the father who demands that leaves be raked once a week, regardless of the next day's wind, or the dictator who restricts civil rights in order to preserve his hold on power. Questioning such authority can be dangerous, but it may be the only way to accomplish change.

Think of the teenager who rebels against raking leaves once a week, only to see his work compounded with each new storm. He can choose one of two paths. He can mouth off to his father, pointing out that parents are, in general, stodgy, silly traditionalists who require labor for labor's sake from their children. He can rage against the power and refuse to work. (He will likely spend time in his room or a weekend without car keys.) An alternative approach would be to proffer arguments, calmly and in a non-confrontational way, that demonstrate how the leaves might be picked up more efficiently on a different schedule. Whether or not the arguments are valid, calm and non-confrontational are the operative mechanics of this approach. In the end, the parent may or may not agree to the son's request. At least there is a possibility that he will. But regardless of the outcome relative to leaf raking, in all probability the teenager will retain car privileges because he questioned with respect for the authority, while still provoking the argument.

Sometimes the risk of asking questions is much greater than the scorn of a professor or the loss of car privileges. Violence has historically worked, at least as often as nonviolence, in changing the role of authority. We want to believe that George Washington and friends were right in the method they ultimately adopted for questioning British rule of the American colonies; the potential reward warranted war. We want to believe that Gandhi was right in his method of freeing India from colonialism because he had the moral strength to face guns with nonaggression. We do not believe that twenty-first-century car bombers and suicide terrorists are right in their approach, in large part because they ignore the rules of traditional warfare and target innocent bystanders, though there is arguably a very fine line that objectively separates some modern terrorists from the guerilla forces of Massachusetts in 1777.

Probing and questioning are preferable to precipitous action. When questioning authority, however, it is best to remember the stream and the rocks. Sometimes the water hits the rock, and sometimes it goes quietly around the obstacle. The only thing that can prevent the water from ultimately winning the battle is for sea level to rise, thus reducing the force of gravity on the flow. The stream will ultimately wear down the rocks, but some of the water molecules are going to get a nasty bump in the process.

Formulating the Scope of a Question

One of the most important aspects of asking questions is to determine whether or not the question can lead to a meaningful answer. This is itself, of course, a question. Is it more important to answer a question quickly or to see where it leads in hopes of finding new worlds of questions to answer? Do you want to complete a doctoral dissertation, or do you want the answer tomorrow, this afternoon, now? This is a fundamental learning skill that can be incorporated in almost any classroom or training setting. At the outset of a project or discussion, teachers and students can discuss and agree the scope of inquiry and a range of possible outcomes.

To foster creative thought, jump quickly from question to answer to new question and new answer. Fly with the creative stimulation and see where it takes you. Binding the process with the sinews of an expected outcome will probably ruin the exercise.

If analysis is your goal, slow down, dwell on the answers, and ponder each assumption and each result. Rigor and investigation will ensure that each step meets with your chosen tests of logic, and that in the end the result will be both satisfying and defensible.

Not to belabor the riparian metaphor, Robert Persig expressed the idea well in *Zen and the Art of Motorcycle Maintenance* when he discussed the times in our lives when we need to be like a river that erodes downward to deepen the valley, and those times when we need to broaden that valley to develop a flat floor, rich in deep, tillable soil. Our ability to question is the sharpest tool we have to cut downward to expose new layers, new territory, new ideas and opportunities, if that is what we wish to do. It is also our best tool to broaden our understanding through thought, analysis, and insight, if that is what we wish to do. We choose different questions at different times, and we get different results.

In our seminar, I related to my students a story from the first real job I ever had with an oceanographic research company. Our business was to map the ocean floor. We were scientists, but we worked for a profit. Our work had to be accurate, but it also had to be done within budget.

One researcher (I will call him John) was routinely given the task of creating bathymetric maps. Bathymetric maps show the depth of the ocean, just as topographic maps show the elevation of land above sea level. Before the era of powerful small computers, maps like this were made by hand, and the work involved as much estimation and art as science. First, John would figure out where the ship had traveled by looking at the navigational records. Second, he would plot the depth of the ocean at locations along the ship's tracks. Third, he would sit back, scratch his head, and worry, sometimes for weeks on end, because the depths where two tracks crossed did not exactly match.

Why not? The instruments that collect the soundings are supposed to be very accurate. They work on the principle of the speed of sound in seawater, which is dependent on the temperature of the water. John would perform the temperature correction, revise his depths, and still the depths did not match.

Why not? The soundings assume that the instrument on the ship is pointing straight down at the sea floor, but this is rarely the case because swells and waves make the ship roll side to side and pitch forward and aft. John would review the ship's log for the days of each track crossing, correct for the maximum deflection due to the swell, and the depths would still not match.

Why not? The track lines assume that we really know where a ship is in the middle of the ocean, and before the days of global positioning satellites, the ship's location might be off by several tens of meters or more. John would review the navigation records, slide the track lines this way and that, looking for a best fit that would answer each track-tie problem, and the inelasticity of time and space would defeat the exercise once again.

John could not bring himself to sign his name to a map that might or might not be inaccurate by one or three or five meters in depth.

As a new manager to the group, I looked at the time it took John to make a map. We wanted to produce the best maps possible, but not at the risk of bankrupting the company in cost overruns. At some point, I thought, you just have to make your best guess, note it for the record, and get on to the next project.

John and I made the next map together. It took us two and a half days from start to finish, and we never had a complaint from the client or the government. The job came in under budget. First set a goal. Then ask questions within the scope of that goal. There may be no bad questions, but some can be a real waste of time.

While my seminar students were not familiar with the details or science of seafloor mapping, they quickly adopted the metaphor of this story as it really deals with the simple relationships of time, resources, and our ability to manage the two in an effective manner. In fact, one of the most significant results of testing this type of instruction was that students were often more quick to grasp the most important, if somewhat less tangible, lessons when presented within an unfamiliar context. Since the context was not important and certainly not something that might lead to an exam, the students were free to focus on the forest of the story's lesson instead of the particular trees of detail, as is common in most classroom settings.

*   *   *   *

The Importance of Questioning Assumptions

In the case of the bathymetric maps, what if John's compulsion had been warranted, if a more rigorous investigation would have uncovered a depth discrepancy that may have jeopardized the safety of a pipeline or the stability of a pier? What if, for the sake of a profitable project, I had precipitously spiked the investigation? Had I thrown out the urchin with the seawater?

Not if we correctly trace our questions and the assumptions that guide them. If you keep track of where you have been, what assumptions you have made, and how these have directed or weighed the results, then you can always backtrack and try a new set of assumptions if new conditions warrant such a quest. In a scientific investigation, this means keeping a good record in the logbook. For a classroom term paper, this means taking good notes. For personal growth and decision-making, this means remembering or noting why you do the things you do. If you ever want to go back and question your assumptions, which you should do frequently, you will know how you got to where you are.

The exercise of retracing or reinvestigating steps in the mental process of decision making involves the power of iterative thinking. Simply, iterative thinking is the process of going back and revisiting or retesting a conclusion with a variety of input data. We can think of this as a constant feedback loop, one of the most important steps in our ability to control the outcome of decisions. Feedback loops recheck the assumptions that led us to an answer in the first place.

In the technology age, many of us are familiar with the adage "garbage in, garbage out." We use it to restrict our blind faith in computers and "black boxes." Our machines may calculate at the speed of light, but the results and answers that they give are only as good as the information that is put in on the front end. How do we know that our own decisions, the answers that we deduce after asking a sequence of questions, are based on valid assumptions? How often do we look back in time and question the foundational assumptions in our personal portfolio of knowledge?

In one of our seminar discussions in 1998, a group of senior high school students discussed the pressures of competing for admission to the top universities. As part of our exercise in questioning, they looked back at how and why they had each arrived at this point of stress in their young lives. Was it parental anxiety? Was it societal or peer pressure? Did they all want to get the best college education that cash and loans could buy in order to get good jobs and be rich?

All of these factors received discussion and support until one student stopped the discussion. With a far-off look in her eye, she said that she could pinpoint the *exact* reason for her being where she was now. In looking back, remembering the few years of her short life, she recalled a particular time in the *third grade* when she had decided to work hard in school in order to get into a good college. As if she were waking up from a dream, she suddenly saw how each life decision that she and her family had made since then, each choice of a class, each team try-out, each choice about how to apportion her valuable time and resources had been built, snowballing, from that one decision in third grade. Her life had been ruled, rightly or wrongly, by the decision of a nine-year-old girl, influenced by passions and information that can only be guessed at in the mist of passed time.

Did this realization mean that she wanted to change her life, even if she could? Not necessarily. She may be completely happy, on balance, with all that has happened since and all that it signifies. But it is not hard to imagine a different set of assumptions, a different path of faith or beliefs that are built on a set of assumptions that may no longer be valid. The young woman had not revisited her baseline assumptions in a very long time; any change in those assumptions now would result in a cataclysmic life change these many years later.

By learning to insert feedback loops into our thought, questioning, and decision-making process, we increase the chance of staying on our desired path. Or, if the path needs to be modified, our midcourse corrections become less dramatic and disruptive.

In the Information Age, the constant need to question assumptions is increasingly critical. Five hundred years ago, most information was self-evident. The cow was either sick or healthy and, if sick, would either die or not after application of a very limited number of potential remedies. The small amount of information available that was not self-evident was accepted on faith, but the total amount and diversity of such information required to live one's life was exceedingly small.

Today the number of sources of information, and the distance between original sources and the information we actually receive is enormous. Nearly all of the information we receive has been filtered through computers, electronic measuring, analyzing, or monitoring devices, audio-visual equipment, third parties, news companies, political spin doctors, and vast distances of time and space. Anyone with a cheap computer and a modem or cable connection can post "information" on the Internet, and only the reader can decide how much weight to give to the posting. If we don't understand the basis for a set of statements or results, why should we believe the conclusions?

Defense against believing garbage is easy. One of the most popular exercises in The Falconer seminar was the day that, without warning, I taught the students the power of devil's advocacy. I asked for a volunteer to share something about which they felt passionately to convince the group that they were right. Hands shot up; we are always eager to convince the world that something about which we care deeply is true. After a short and always vigorous lesson on capital punishment or abortion or recycling or the school dress code from the student, I then insisted that they argue, *just as passionately*, the opposite. The response was always, initially, the same: "I can't." And then the challenge set in, and in every case, the students were effective at countering their own deeply held beliefs. And also in every case, when I asked a second student to undertake the same exercise, everyone in the room jumped to volunteer. There was an immediate and seemingly liberating excitement in knowing, suddenly, that you are smart enough to know both sides of a question.

Argue *against* yourself and your beliefs with all of the vigor, ferocity, and faith with which you argue *for* yourself and your beliefs. At first you will be tempted to argue weakly because the devil's advocate role is more difficult than believing we are right in the first place; it takes us out of our comfort zone. If you resist this temptation, play the role truly, like a great lawyer who is paid to argue a position in which she may not believe, you will test the underlying assumptions and sources of your positions. If, in the end, you can out-argue the devil, your position will have a vastly more secure foundation.

Trace arguments backward. Question assumptions. Always. It's the only way to prevent garbage in, garbage out.

Sun Tzu on Questioning

If questioning is an important step in our path, it seems that *The Art of War* should contain additional references to the process and significance of the art of questioning. Indeed, we note several statements that seem to specifically discuss the importance of critical examination and inquiry. Fortunately, Mr. Sun arrives back just as we have finished earmarking a few of his comments, as we wish to ask him to quality check our interpretation. He is carrying a stout long bow and has a quiver of sleek arrows hung across his back. We ask if he practices archery. He replies that, yes, archery is like poetry to him, and in fact archery and questioning have quite a bit in common. We spread out our manuscript before him and point to the passages that we have noted.

Sun Tzu writes: *The art of war is of vital importance to the State. It is a matter of life and death, a road either to safety or to ruin. Hence it is a subject of inquiry, which can on no account be neglected.*

This means that facing challenges, both problems and opportunities, is vital to personal success. This is the arena in which we can grow, excel, create, and expand. Without these challenges, we wither. Because of this importance, it is equally vital that we examine the way in which we meet the challenges by questioning our path from the outset.

Sun Tzu writes: *If the enemy leaves the door open, you must rush in. At first, then, exhibit the coyness of a maiden, until the enemy gives you an opening; afterwards emulate the rapidity of a running hare and it will be too late for the enemy to oppose you.*

This means that you should not procrastinate when you see how to proceed. Be proactive, not reactive. The first step in the proactive pursuit of a solution is to ask the questions that will open the way ahead. Since questions inevitably lead to more questions, this first step is the most important at maximizing the number of potential solutions. Once the door of options is open, you have a better chance of finding a way to a satisfactory conclusion.

Sun Tzu writes: *To lift an autumn hair is no sign of great strength; to see the sun and moon is no sign of sharp sight; to hear the noise of thunder is no sign of a quick ear.*

This means that easy problems are easy to solve; don't make an easy problem more difficult. The answers are often self-evident, but the rewards may be limited. Subtle issues are more difficult to approach and require persistence and often creativity. Asking questions that have not been asked before or turning old questions in a new way can be a difficult but critical first step.

Mr. Sun says that many more of his passages also contain an inherent reference to the role of questioning since questioning is our most cherished tool. Perhaps another way to frame the issue is that *resources and abilities are like the arrows in a quiver; the desire and willingness to ask questions are like a long bow. Without the bow, the arrows are just a lot of wood, feathers, and sharp little points.*

"Congratulations on understanding the importance of questioning. You are now ready to take the critical step of questioning your self in relation to the world around you," says Mr. Sun. "All of the investigation in the world comes to naught if we don't know how our own views affect and determine the outcome of the answers. In fact, I'm on my way to a rather unique pond in the middle of the forest that is famous for its clarity of reflection, so we will reserve our discussion of self-awareness until a bit later.

"I once wrote," Mr. Sun continues, "'hence is it not enough to put one's trust in the tethering of horses, and the burying of chariot wheels in the ground,' and I am glad to see that you have correctly interpreted its meaning in modern terms. If we are too closely tied to our beliefs, if our sources of information are slave to forces about which we know little, if we are not flexible enough to constantly challenge and question the underpinnings of our knowledge foundations, then certainly we will not reach our goal. Maybe I just should have written 'garbage in, garbage out'!"

We tell Mr. Sun that we prefer his poetic way with words, even if they are hard for us to interpret so many years after they were written.

"I have somewhat the same problem," he says, as he walks calmly off into the forest in search of his mysterious pond. "I have not found the answer to your *koan* about gravity and concepts and principles. First I think it is one, and then the other, and then somewhere in between. It sounds like something your Mr. Usher would tempt his young students with, though I'm sure that he does not need to reach quite so far to come up with interesting questions to ask. This question has cut into my sleep considerably the last few nights."

We smile, thinking that there is, in fact, some little balance in the world.

Step 2: The Boundaries of Subjectivity and Objectivity

Quality is the mystery that subjectivity and objectivity can't answer.
Colin Jemmot, Falconer Class of 2000

We find ourselves seated beside a small pond, no doubt the one to which Mr. Sun so recently referred, buried deeply in a thick forest of pungent pine, stately hemlock, palm-splayed fern, and heathery moss. Somewhere beyond the trees, a small waterfall tinkles soprano and breathy feathers ripple up in the treetops. The breeze does not penetrate the canopy, and the pond is as rigid as a sheet of glass welded into the bank, the reflections so sharp that we clench the ground from vertigo.

Mr. Sun sits with his back to a deeply eroded log at the edge of the pond and looks at us across the delicate reflections. His longbow and sword lie on the moss in front of him. From where we sit across the pond, it appears that there are two inverted warriors joined at his crossed legs.

"I wrote 'Hence the saying: If you know the enemy and know yourself, you need not fear the result of a hundred battles. If you know yourself but not the enemy, for every victory gained you will also suffer a defeat. If you know neither the enemy nor yourself, you will succumb in every battle.' Knowledge of self is one of the most important ideas in *The Art of War*. It is imperative that you know your own self, your strengths and weaknesses, and your own worldview, or you cannot hope to fight life's battles. But I should have looked more deeply at this issue of self-knowledge. There are subtleties that create who and what we are. These can be explored and developed, and we are stronger strategists for it. I have had a couple of millennia now to contemplate this question, and there is a great deal more to say. For now, though, why don't you go off with Mr. Usher and your other guides, and when you have explored on your own, I will be here and we can talk again."

We take our leave and Mr. Sun fades back into the still life of the pond.

*   *   *   *

The Lesson of the Table

Sometimes in the late spring, when humid air invades the Children's valley from the south, the sky turns a misty shade of gray white with the horizon between sky and the mountains invisible for days at a time. It was on such a day, the sky a vaulted bowl of bottomless haze that made one feel like gravity might give up and one could fall upwards with lack of direction, that the Children first encountered the Table.

As usual the Children lined up for class, and as usual they all jostled each other and gabbed noisily for a minute or two before the class bell rang, and as usual they all took off their sweatshirts and caps as they entered Mr. Usher's class. But as they did so they saw something unusual indeed; instead of their orderly rows of familiar desks and chairs, the entire center of the room was taken up by one enormous wooden table with their small student chairs spread around it like little piglets nestled up to their big fat mother.

Mr. Usher stood at one corner of the table and smiled at the obvious discomfort of the Children as they surveyed this change in their classroom.

"It's okay," Mr. Usher called to them, over the murmur of questions, mostly about how such a large table got into the room in the first place. "Take a seat anywhere. Class will be a little different today."

So the Children each found a seat, with all of the usual bother and argument about who would sit next to whom that always happens when we don't have assigned places to be. Mr. Usher let them go on for a while, and then sorted the last few of the Children into open seats and asked for quiet.

"We have a special task today, or at least it will start today. For some of us this discussion is the start of something that may last a lifetime. We each have to decide a single fundamental question about how we view the world around us."

Now the Children of course had heard such strange statements from Mr. Usher in the past, but even so, several of them immediately raised their hands.

"What do you mean 'how do we view the world'?" Scott asked. "I view the world with my eyes. And I sure can't see the whole world, no matter how hard I look." Many of the other Children nodded in agreement with Scott.

"'View the world' is an expression," Mr. Usher replied patiently. "It means that each one of us sees some things differently than other people do. This can be something simple like the way someone who is colorblind sees a field of flowers compared to how someone with normal vision sees the same field. It can be more complicated, like how we each like a different food or each choose a different way to think about God or each describe a rose with different words. Today we are going to try to find out if there are some things in the world that we all can agree on, or if there may be nothing at all that we call can agree on."

The Children all looked even more puzzled than usual when Mr. Usher started with one of his sometimes-strange ideas. He just chuckled and told them that in the end they would understand, at least as much as was possible, which made most of the Children raise their eyebrows even more.

"First let me read you two definitions," said Mr. Usher, opening the heavy leather-bound dictionary that he kept on the shelf behind his desk.

"The first is for the word subjective: 'characteristic of or belonging to reality as perceived rather than as independent of mind; experience or knowledge as conditioned by personal mental states.'

"The second is for the word *objective*: 'an object, phenomenon or condition in the realm of sensible experience independent of individual thought and perceptible to all observers; having reality independent of the mind.'

"Now those are some pretty big words and concepts, so let's think them over and see if we can all understand what they mean. Remember our discussions about being prepared to learn: it does not help us to talk about things unless we are pretty sure we are all talking about the same things."

"I think the first definition means that things are as we choose to see them," said Chantal. "If we think something is beautiful or ugly, or if we think something is smooth or rough, that's the way it really is."

"Very good," replied Mr. Usher. "The key phrases here are 'perceived' and 'independent of mind.' If we take a *subjective* view of the world, we are stating that everything is 'subject' to our own point of view."

Several hands shot up; Mr. Usher called on Matt.

"That's nuts! There are a lot of things in the world that are not determined by how we view them. Sandpaper is rough and peach skin is fuzzy and glass is smooth no matter what. I agree more with the second definition. It means that things are the way they are, regardless of what you or I might think about them. We can see and measure and describe the world around us. Maybe we can't agree on what is beautiful and what is ugly, but we can sure agree on what is round and what is square."

After the Children talked back and forth for a while, Mr. Usher quieted them down.

"You seem to have a good understanding of the definitions of *subjective* and *objective*. These two words describe two very different ways of looking at the universe in which we live. You have correctly understood that a person who takes a wholly *subjective* viewpoint believes that all of reality is a function of his or her perceptions. In contrast, a person who takes a wholly *objective* viewpoint believes that things are they way they are no matter who or what acts as the observer.

"So let's try something," Mr. Usher continued. "Everyone who thinks he or she has a more *subjective* view of the world move down to this end of the table," extending his left arm, "and everyone who thinks he or she has a more *objective* view of the world, move down to this end," pointing to his right.

The Children all wrinkled their foreheads and chattered at each other, but in a very few minutes they all had changed seats and were organized around the wide, heavy wooden table according to their general worldview. There were a few more children towards the right end of the table than the left, but not so many that the neutral observer would notice.

"Thank you, class," began Mr. Usher again. "You have now all taken a critical step in your lives. You have clearly stated a personal bias towards one of two completely opposite points of view. Neither point of view is right or wrong, but it is extremely important that you know how you view the world. Your ability to find and solve problems and ultimately to struggle less on the road to happiness requires that you know some fundamental things about yourselves, and this is one of them."

"Now," he continued, "here comes the fun part. Let's put some meat on these bones that we are calling *subjectivity* and *objectivity*. Let's see what they really mean to us. Everyone push his or her chair away from the table. Good. Stay seated. Close your eyes and keep them closed. Keep your hands in your lap. Don't move and don't make a sound. Okay? Everyone's eyes closed?"

The Children all nodded their heads.

"Now, without moving or opening your eyes, someone prove to me that there is a table in the room."

The Children were so quiet you could have heard a butterfly sigh from one end of the room to the other.

"We can't!" yelled Scott finally, with more than a little frustration seeping in. "But we all know it's there because it was a minute ago and no one has moved it."

"Well," said Mr. Usher, "without moving or opening your eyes can anyone tell us if the table is smooth or rough, or what color it is?"

"It's smooth and brown," said Matt.

"Or at least it was when we closed our eyes," said Chantal.

"Without moving or opening your eyes," said Mr. Usher, "in other words without using your senses, can anyone *prove* to the rest of us that the table even exists?"

"Of course it exists," Matt almost yelled. "It was just there a minute ago. It can't have stopped existing."

"Prove it," said Mr. Usher. "No eyes, no ears, no touch, no moving. Can you prove that the table exists?"

Of course no one could.

"Open your eyes and then close them quickly," Mr. Usher directed. "Now what can you say about the existence of the table?"

"It is there when our eyes are open, but we can't actually prove it is there when our eyes are closed," said Chantal.

"What about the rest of the room?" asked Mr. Usher. "In fact, what about everything in the room except the chair under your bottom and the floor under your feet. When you sit still and close your eyes and pretend that you can't hear the robins singing outside the window, can you prove that anything physical actually exists?"

No one could.

"Well, *I* can prove the table exists," said Scott. "I will sit here all day, hitting the table with my hand. Every time I bring my hand down it will hit a solid table and not thin air. Every single time. If the table did not exist, my hand would hit nothing but air all the time or some of the time. I'll even sit here all week to prove it if I have to. Of course, the table exists. It's right there."

"How about right after you stop hitting it, or in between hits?" asked Chantal. "Can you prove it exists at a time when you are not looking at it or touching it?"

"No," said Scott, "but I have no reason to believe it does not exist."

The other Children had been sitting quietly, listening to the give and take of their classmates.

"Let's go back to the definitions," said Mr. Usher. "Think about the meaning of those terms. Does anyone want to move their seat from one end of the table to the other? Has anyone changed her or his mind about how he or she views the world?"

After a few seconds several of the Children moved from the "objective" end to the "subjective" end. Some raised and lowered their hands over the table as if waiting to see if the table would suddenly disappear.

Mr. Usher continued. "What we have learned with this simple exercise is that we at least have to consider the possibility that the subjective view of the world is correct, even for objects and phenomena that seem irrefutably constant. We really are at the mercy of our senses. If we take away our senses, we can prove very little indeed. And since my senses are mine, and your senses are yours, it is difficult if not impossible to prove, beyond all doubt, that we are experiencing the same reality.

"We have overcome this in the everyday world by inventing measures and rules and criteria that we share amongst ourselves and try to agree upon in order to describe the world around us. We invent the 'inch' or 'liter' or 'red' or 'sweet,' and most of all, we agree to not worry ourselves that when our eyes are shut or our other senses are closed off the table might blink out of existence and our books fall on the floor. We have adopted our objective reality because subjective reality would be just too cumbersome an existence."

Matt raised his hand. "Why do we care about this? If for all practical purposes the table is 'there,' and it is only a question of philosophy, why is it so important to us?"

"Excellent question, Matt," replied Mr. Usher. "Maybe the best question since that thing about Gravity, come to think of it.

"If the universe is completely objective, then there are things we can't change, no matter how hard we try. They are fixed, either by natural laws or by God or fate or some other set of forces about which we have, at best, only partial understanding. We know we only have partial understanding because we keep finding out new things, so by definition we are always at least somewhat wrong, and we can't ever be completely right.

"If the universe exists subject to our own perception of it, then nothing is fixed except our understanding of our Self; we may in fact be the equivalent of God or fate ourselves, and just not know it. We may well have the capability of knowing everything once we figure out that we are the ones controlling reality.

"These are two completely different starting points, and as a wise little girl named Dorothy once said, it's good to start at the beginning if you want to get to the end.

"If we want to understand the world around us, we first need to know ourselves and how that Self influences or interacts with the exterior world. We need to understand the relationship between Self and everything else."

David had been sitting quietly, listening to the entire discussion. He raised his hand timidly.

"If the table might not exist, then everyone else in this room might not exist. You all might just be a creation of my senses. And if that were true, I would just be a creation of someone else's senses. All of this could just be a dream."

"That's ridiculous," said Matt. "I know I am here and you know you are here. And my hand hurts, so the table is here, too."

Mr. Usher laughed and applauded both David and Matt. "You have both proven the main point of this exercise. Regardless of right or wrong, the two of you would go about the process of solving problems and evaluating opportunities in *very* different ways. We need to know that ahead of time, or we shall lose our way quickly and waste a great deal of our precious resources in the process. One thing that *is* important, however, is that you should each accept the fact that the other *may* be right, and you may be wrong. Acceptance that something is possible opens a lot of doors to creative thinking."

And with that, Mr. Usher told the Children to take an early recess, and that the table would be moved out of the classroom the next day. The Children gathered up their sweaters and caps and went out into the schoolyard, where the sky had not cleared at all, and the horizon remained hazier than usual with a hint of clearing in the west. The Children befuddled and annoyed most of the rest of the students that recess by walking up to the jungle gym, closing their eyes, slapping at the bars, and laughing out loud.

*   *   *   *

The exercise of the table is simple and can be undertaken by any class of students of almost any grade level. Younger students may not grasp the philosophical issues, but even they can recognize that, lacking our senses, it us hard to be certain about the world around us. As we undertook this short exercise in The Falconer seminar, in a number of cases, students underwent fundamental and visceral revisions in their worldviews in just fifteen or twenty minutes. It quickly became a shared metaphor that the students recall years later.

The philosophical conundrum of subjectivity and objectivity has been with us at least since the time of the ancient Greek philosophers. While this duality has tumbled through human consciousness for over two thousand years, physical science, the interpretation of the tangible universe in which we live and operate, has progressed dramatically in the last century. Twentieth-century physics places some dramatic constraints on this fundamental philosophical concept. Since we must ask ourselves, as Mr. Usher asked his Children, to define our own worldview as a critical step towards self-knowledge, we should avail ourselves of current scientific paradigms.

In order to understand the implication of modern physics on our personal metaphysics, we need a brief discussion of quantum mechanics. We refer the interested student to the far more exhaustive, elegant, and eminently understandable treatises on the congruence of physics and philosophy: *The Dancing Wu Li Masters* by Gary Zukav and *The Tao of Physics* by Fritjof Capra.

From the mid-1600s until the earliest years of the twentieth century, Newtonian physics encapsulated our best understanding of the laws of the physical universe. Newton accurately described the actions of the observable universe, from planets to apples, from springs to billiard balls to bicycle wheels. None of that has changed. Newton's fundamental laws that we all learn in our high school physics classes are as valid today as they were nearly four centuries ago.

In the early part of the twentieth century, a number of primarily European physicists contributed to a new branch of physics that defines and describes what takes place at subatomic scales. For most of us, it would seem that physics on a scale that is too small to directly observe would not have a great deal of meaning. We would be wrong. This branch of physics, quantum mechanics, provides the foundation for pretty much all of modern science, from genetic engineering to astrophysics to nuclear energy to weaponry.

Quantum mechanics essentially says that nature comes in very small pieces or building blocks, so small that we cannot directly observe them. We know the pieces exist because of how they interact with each other. We also can prove that these pieces do *not* act like the larger, observable parts of the Newtonian universe.

The details of quantum mechanical interactions are not relevant to our discussion. What is relevant is how we attempt to observe these interactions, and what this attempt tells us about the relationship between our Self, the observer, and that which we attempt to model or define. One of the pioneers of quantum mechanics was a young German physicist named Werner Heisenberg. After studying the results of many subatomic experiments and applying the most advanced mathematical modeling of the day, Heisenberg posited what has become known and universally accepted as a fundamental paradigm of science, the Uncertainty Principle. This principle states that as we explore deep into the subatomic realm, it is not possible to accurately and simultaneously describe the two fundamental properties of small particles: their position and their momentum. The more we try to know about one aspect of the particle, the less we can know about the other. This is not a limitation on the sensitivity of our instruments; it is a limitation on our sensory observations themselves at these scales. The result is that we cannot actually define and articulate with any degree of certainty that a subatomic particle exists at a certain point in space and time. The best we can do is to predict the *probability* that the particle will exist at this point in space and time. Matter, therefore, at the foundation level and to the best of our observational abilities, does not exist except as a probability.

There are a number of basic philosophical ramifications to the Uncertainty Principle. First, we the observer are forced to choose how to observe the particles, thus defining the outcome of the observation. We cannot prove that the particles would not be completely different, reflecting a different set of probabilities, if we had chosen to observe them in a different fashion. By setting the observation parameters, we have pre-judged how the particle will appear.

Second, the very act of observing a subatomic particle changes the particle itself. We cannot make observations at this scale without introducing energy into the system that is far greater than the energy of the particles themselves. In essence, we knock the particles about, thus polluting whatever it was that we wanted to know about them in the first place. We, the observers, have become an overwhelmingly important part of what we are trying to objectively study.

These two aspects of quantum mechanics essentially define that at the subatomic level we cannot objectively and dispassionately observe the physical universe. According to the current state of physics, this can never change. And most, if not all, of modern science is either built upon, or at a minimum agrees with, quantum mechanics.

Therefore, using our simple definitions of subjectivity and objectivity, we have to conclude that we cannot objectively define the building blocks of the physical universe. The subatomic world, at a minimum, exists subject to our views of it and is not objectively the same to all observers.

Scientific investigation has come a long way since the days of Heisenberg, Bohr, Einstein, and others. It is likely that our children and grandchildren will be as familiar with the physics of infinitely small strings of matter and energy that define the boundaries of multiple parallel realities as we were at their age with the action and reaction of billiard balls on a frictionless surface. The boundaries of physics and philosophy grow fuzzier, not sharper. If anything, the uncertainty first postulated by Heisenberg grows more uncertain, not less. Physics demands that the universe is a highly subjective, inconstant place.

This brings us to Kevin.

I had a friend in college named Kevin. This is a short look at a brief part of Kevin's life, or at least what I saw and understood of it. I told the story of Kevin to my seminar students, and, for many of them, it is another of the stories that they remember years later; it presents the listener or reader with a fundamental challenge to what we think of as a c-based worldview. At the end you will have the same three choices about Kevin that my students did, and what he means to us and to our model.

The first option is that I am telling you a series of self-serving fables designed to shape your view of the world to my own. I can promise you that this is not the case, but if you think I am lying, such an assurance is of little consequence.

The second option is that Kevin's story is true in its difficult-to-accept entirety. While *I* happen to think this is so, it seems a large leap of faith for the reader, who wasn't there, to make.

The third is that Kevin's story, or some part of it, *may* be true, that some things that we cannot fully understand or rationally demonstrate *may*, nonetheless, be real. In this eventuality, it does not really matter if the actual events of Kevin's story are true or not because the story of Kevin would be a metaphor for all that is possible, however improbable.

Having said that, all that follows really happened. Really.

Kevin is his real first name, but we shall not use his last as he still lives in a quiet town south of San Francisco and is a responsible father and agreeable, if somewhat secretive, middle-aged man. Kevin was always tight-lipped until well after he believed that you had both the ability and the desire to understand.

Kevin did not surf or chase girls like the rest of us. His wild straw-colored Einstein-like hair and wire-rimmed glasses framed a pale Irish face atop an academic's thin body, rolled up plaid sleeves, and faded blue jeans. At least in his freshman year, Kevin was a double major in philosophy and physics, the reflection of his unique searches and oft-twisted concerns about the duality of subjectivity and objectivity. Kevin was not a social crawler of the dormitory niche, no freshman frat boy, but he was smart and focused, and we all respected him for the passion of his introspection.

For most of one quarter, Kevin worried about Xeno's Paradox, which states that if you are traveling from point A to point B you must necessarily travel half of the distance before traveling all of the distance; from that halfway point, you must again travel half of the remaining distance. If you continue to do so you will never reach point B. At lunch, sitting on the patio with our yogurt and apples, Kevin would get out of this chair, take a few steps, then a few smaller ones, and then sit back down with the stern frustration that Xeno might apply not only to physical motion but also to mental travels and explorations of the soul. How, he asked, can I ever understand something new if I can only get halfway to the answer?

For another quarter Kevin worried mightily about the expansion of the universe and what happens when the expansion stops. At the same time, he was jousting with the possibility that the universe switches on and off every time we blink our eyes, and trying to reconcile the physics of expansion and blinking of all of creation with what he considered the ephemeral, and possibly false, world of everyday reality.

And then one sunny day in the spring of Kevin's junior year, a friend came back from visiting with a dwarfish yoga teacher down in the desert of Mexico. The teacher had instructed her eager students to stand in the rays of the morning sun, absorbing energy through one upturned palm and passing it gently on to Mother Earth through the other down-turned palm. Hearing the story, we all enthusiastically closed our eyes, stood with arms stretched wide and palms appropriately turned, and concentrated as hard as we could to feel the flux. Of course we failed, our sore arms failing us after a minute or two. Kevin stood up, stretched his arms out, and held them there for a quarter of an hour and then, with a small noiseless smile, slowly rotated his up palm to down and vice versa. After another fifteen minutes, he let out a contented sigh, sat down, and told us that, yes, such a tangible and tingling flow of energy should invigorate even the coldest heart.

At some point Kevin must have decided we were worthy of a fuller measure of his trust. One evening Kevin came into my brother's dorm room where my brother and a friend were studying for a biology test. Kevin asked my brother to take a seat at his desk chair and for the friend to sit on the bed and watch. Kevin asked my brother to close his eyes and let him know every time he (my brother) felt a tap on his back, which he did as dutifully witnessed by the friend on the bed, except that the friend confirmed that Kevin never actually touched my brother at all. He gathered his fingers together and shook them at my brother's back, a foot or so away, as one might toss a pinch of salt into a saucepan. Every time Kevin "tapped," my brother said "now," and the friend on the bed stared dry mouthed as if the sea were parting in front of a skinny prophet. Then Kevin placed his hands on either side of my brother's head, several inches from each ear, and my brother howled out as colors exploded in front of his closed eyes, and then disappeared, and then exploded again as Kevin moved his hands to and from the sides of his head. After two or three passes, Kevin collapsed lazily in the corner and told his wide-eyed witnesses that that was enough for one night.

My friends and I talked to Kevin a lot about energy and its relationship to mass, to us, to consciousness, to God, and Kevin patiently assured us that shooting energy out of his hands was just something that happened when he really focused on it. After all, weren't we all just a quantum mechanical admixture of energy and matter? What's the big deal? Why learn the science and then reject the practical application?

And then something in Kevin began to sag, to bend, to lose support under the weight of his being. His enthusiasm dried up, his introspection turned critical, and his concern with a mental Xeno trap grew like an impenetrable wall to any happiness that might lie ahead. Every turn of his questioning seemed to lead him to dead ends that held only dissatisfaction. It was as if he were struggling though a swamp of over-knowledge and could not find a spot of dry ground to just sit and enjoy the day. He very clearly, very rationally, and very calmly told us that he probably needed to kill himself, that he had thought long and hard about it, and since most forms of suicide selfishly left a god-awful mess that others would have to clean up, he planned to climb into a double layer of garbage bags and fall off the top floor of the ten-story dormitory building.

How do you convince the smartest guy, the guy who commands energy and visualizes universal expansion that he is missing the simplest of all answers? We talked and talked to Kevin, told him that he was wrong, that we loved him, that he couldn't cop out that easily, but finally one afternoon we were pretty sure he was going to do it. My brother and I went home and promised each other that at nine o'clock we would both meditate as hard as we could on Kevin, to try to send some positive waves on some astral pathway that might bypass Kevin's rejection of both logical and emotional arguments.

Fighting off the premonition of bad news the next day, god-awful mess or not, we did our best with mental visions of light and positive thoughts. Next morning on my way to class, here comes Kevin bouncing along the walkway through a grove of old eucalyptus trees and smiling like he had just cleared the pot betting to an inside straight. I asked him how he was doing, and he said he was great, that the previous evening at nine o'clock sharp everything had jumped into focus; his ideas of suicide puffed away like a bad dream, and he could not understand his earlier fixations, walls, and depressions. I told him about our meditations, and he acted surprised and kind of touched that we had actually been so concerned; he thanked me matter-of-factly, strolled off to class, and that's the last we ever heard about it.

What are the lessons of Kevin, and how do they relate to quantum mechanics, the Uncertainty Principle, and our worldview? If we believe in Kevin's "power," miracles, angels, quantum theory, or any number of other relatively unexplainable phenomena, we must accept that the world, to a greater or lesser extent, depending on our abilities, is what we choose to make of it. We allow that there is a great deal that we don't know or cannot explain that is possible, if not probable, yet beyond objective proof. We also allow that the vast majority of us will likely never be able to choose our own perception of the universe, but this does not mean it is impossible to do so. If we believe that the indications of quantum mechanics should stay in the subatomic realm and do *not* have relevance to problems in the real world, we reduce the complexity, but also the flexibility and number, of our options.

There is a fundamental difference between those who accept absolute subjectivity as part of their worldview and definition of self, and those who do not. They will address problems and seek solutions in supremely different ways with vastly different desired outcomes and goals. They will create and manage the tests of life as differently as the Children viewed the conundrum of the table. Both can be equally successful, but goals and outcomes will likely be very different.

*   *   *   *

We find ourselves back at the pond, and Mr. Sun has not budged an inch. It's hard to tell how long we have been gone, but given the current subject matter, it hardly seems either critical or relevant. We wait politely for Mr. Sun to sense our presence, though with some fear that this could take a long time.

Our fears are baseless. "In the Lesson of the Table, Mr. Usher directed the attention of his Children on the duality of subjectivity and objectivity," says Mr. Sun, "yet clearly there is much more to knowing ourselves in a strategic sense than knowing where we stand on this single continuum. I wonder if you would explain why you have not delved into the examination of the self's other strengths and weaknesses?"

"Gladly," we respond. "There are two reasons. First, the bookshelves are already more than well stocked with manuals of advice on how we can find our own strengths and weaknesses. Many of these are quite excellent, though one can also find tomes that purport to relate color preferences to the deepest inner working of our souls.

"The primary reason is that we don't want our students to focus, particularly at an early age, on what they think they may or may not be good at. It becomes a self-fulfilling prophecy: students who are weak in analytical skills in an early math class feel they will never be good at analysis. Students who can't draw a stick figure if spotted two legs and an arm think their sensitive sides are underwhelming. It's nonsense, but it happens.

"Skills and talents, that which we think of as strategic strengths, can be learned, leased, acquired, developed. What is much harder to learn is *passion*. Fiery drive to pursue *something* in life is the key to becoming a warrior. With enough passion and motivation, the rest will come.

"So we have asked all of our students what they are passionate about. They list the death penalty, abortion, curing disease, astronomy, or the nature of gravity. They are driven by questions of faith, morality, the social compact, science, science fiction, and exploration. Then for each passion, we start asking the question 'why do you care?' What we have found is that if you start with a passion, whatever it is, and keep asking 'why' enough times, almost everyone will arrive at a fundamental point of their worldview that is grounded in faith. And the duality we have discussed lies at the heart of faith. Try it; 'why' is a very surgical little word."

Mr. Sun nods, not necessarily in agreement, but he has heard and listened to our argument. He ponders for a few minutes, seems to mentally file the issue away for further contemplation, and then directs his attention to us once again. "Before we finish our metaphysical discussions," says Mr. Sun, opening his eyes and peering over the still water towards our sitting stone, "I thought I should point out that your relationship to me in this book is *highly* subjective. I lived the vast majority of my life as a soldier and war consultant, and only tangentially could call myself a poet, writer, artist, or falconer. You choose to see me in these alternative roles because you want to emphasize the non-combative relevance of my doctrine. Nothing wrong with that, and I am happy to participate in this twist since I think the whole war thing has been a bit overemphasized. But you should be completely up front with your own subjective filters and how they help to generate the outcome."

We nod in agreement but, since there was not a question, remain silent.

"When I was young," Mr. Sun continues, "my teacher told me 'go to the pond deep in the forest and you will find your self in its stillness.' I went and looked deeply into the mirror of this pond and of course saw myself reflected back. For years I looked at my reflection. I think my teacher laughed at me behind my back. I finally understood the true meaning of his direction. Of course he meant for me to seek the stillness of the pond in my mind and spirit, and thereby come to know my self.

"I have spent many, many hours meditating here by this pond in hopes of getting past your duality of subjectivity and objectivity. One would think that, given a deep enough experience of one's true nature, this duality would dissolve. I have come to think that such dissolution may not be possible for me, at least in this lifetime.

"Your friend Kevin gives us an interesting milepost. We tend to reserve the manipulation of physical laws to saints and other workers of miracles. Yet you do not describe a saint. If your story of Kevin is true, it means that some people have a clearer understanding of the universe than others. Perhaps he meditated a lot by a pond when he was young; perhaps not. We all have our work to do. I shall at least try to learn from him and not contemplate suicide.

"It is said that one definition of God is that entity which is omnipresent, omniscient, and omnipotent. Perhaps another definition would be that God is that entity for which true objectivity is reserved. For the rest of us, no matter how intelligent or enlightened we may become, we shall always be strained through the filters of our own subjectivity.

"Perhaps between the two of us we have crafted a new postulate:

In order to have complete self–knowledge, the warrior must choose: he and God are one; he and God may some day become one; he and God will never become one; there is no God; he does not know but will seek this knowledge. The only other option is that he does not care, which is not a valid option for the true warrior."

Step 3:
Understanding the System

"Imagination plus creativity equals success. Sounds like something from a fortune cookie!"
Albertina Antonini, Falconer Class of 2000

Two very different kinds of individuals are drawn to interdisciplinary work: those who are curious, well informed, and prone to make well-motivated leaps; and those who spurn orderly linear thinking and are attracted to leaps.
Howard Gardner, *Five Minds for the Future*

The System. In the 1960s, The System referred to that Big Brother body of entrenched powers that ran our lives from a murky den: government, corporations, special interest groups. In the 1980s, news wires brought us stories of the "systematic" destruction of the Brazilian rain forests, a mechanism somehow different and more insidious than non-systematic destruction of rain forests. In the 1990s, a systems analyst became a highly sought-after computer engineer who understands the mysterious pathways of circuits, electricity, software, and black boxes that make computers do what we want them to do.

What do these disparate uses of the word "system," and so many others that we could contemplate, have in common, and why should we care?

"Interdependent group ... forming a unified whole ... a group under the influence of related forces ... an assemblage of substances ..." The dictionary definitions offer a picture that is justifiably broad enough to include a wide range of organized groupings, from family, friends, companies, schools, and political organizations to test tubes, swamps, NATO, planetary groups, and philosophical concepts. In fact, any group of interrelated individual components reflects similar characteristics of a system. Because they share common characteristics, we can study and begin to understand their behavior using specific, defined strategies.

We must analyze systems because, simply, *we cannot defeat our enemy without first knowing him.* The essence of problem solving is designing strategies based on the unique set of relationships posed by the problem itself as well as on our desired outcome. Therefore, an accurate definition of the problem components is essential for success. As we will see later, Sun Tzu recognized this as knowing "the ground" before battle.

A word of warning: this is a long chapter. True understanding that you earn for yourself is the steepest part of our climb. A few people are just lucky; they will find happiness in life no matter what. Most of us, whether we know it or not, *create* opportunities for happiness, and that creation requires the effort of truly understanding, of *knowing*, what is going on in the world around us. This is the sweat equity we must invest, where theory and words can't replace hard work. The great part is that this method works whether you are trying to figure out a complicated ecosystem, the ins and outs at a new job, a tough problem in class, or the generational politics of your new in-laws. Hang in there and before you know it we will have deduced some straightforward tools to make the complex understandable.

We want to launch right into our discussion of how one can understand, both quantitatively and qualitatively, the myriad systems we find about us, but we are pulled into an odd room of discomforting geometry. The center of the room is an equilateral triangle, and in the center of the triangle is a triangular table, open in the middle. The sides of the room seem to push off in all directions, repeating the angular motif, but the lighting in the corners is poor, and the distal portions of the room fade into a broken kaleidoscope of repeated reflections. Mr. Sun is seated on a spinning stool in the middle of the open triangular table.

One side of the table holds a large chessboard, though no one plays opposite Mr. Sun. On another side of the table, computer screens flash stock quotes from financial markets on three continents. The third side of the table is covered with maps and charts and satellite photographs of weather patterns swirling across the northern hemisphere. Mr. Sun slowly turns from one side of the table to the next. At first it seems odd to us that he should be studying any of these materials since none of them existed when Mr. Sun was *really* alive, but we've pretty much gotten past that dissonance; Mr. Sun does not seem terribly constrained by time or space. He looks up from the stock ticker where the value of Microsoft has just reached another all-time high, shakes his head, and asks us to sit with him for a while.

"I'm glad to see that you have made it this far," he says. "Once you prepare yourself, and know your personal perspective, it's time to get to the meat of the matter. Knowledge of how and why things work is the key. I understand that one of your very bright high school students actually said that he would 'trade a lot of knowledge for a little bit of wisdom.' Very good. I couldn't have said it more clearly myself.

"My old manuscript has many, many references to knowledge and systems, and the importance of combining the two. I recall writing 'Ponder and deliberate before you make a move.' In our lexicon, the armed struggle is merely our attempt to understand and face a challenge, problem, or opportunity. Action, the making of decisions, should be reserved until you have completely understood what it is that you are facing. You call this a 'system,' and I suppose that is a good word to use.

"I have many more references to assessment, but it's better you look first on your own, and then we can discuss my views on the subject. Start as a child would and build on each step. None of it will make sense at the beginning, but all of it will make sense in the end. In fact, I suggest you visit with Mr. Usher for a few days and see how even a child can become an expert at studying and analyzing the world around us."

With that Mr. Sun turns back to his table, attacks his invisible opponent's queen with a potentially suicidal bishop, checks a swirling low pressure system moving southward out of the Gulf of Alaska, and sells half of his position in Microsoft.

*   *   *   *

The Lesson of the Forest

One blustery fall day just after Halloween, the leaves were mostly off the trees, and the grass had already turned a dry brown, as it does just a few weeks before the long winter sets in. The sound of a child crying pierced the schoolyard. Two children walked huddled together, one's arm around the other, from the direction of the school office back towards the classrooms. The sound of crying had also carried into Mr. Usher's room; in the blink of an eye, he stopped talking and writing on the chalkboard about fractions and went outside to find out who was crying and why. He found Teresa and Derrick walking back to his class (for they were two of Mr. Usher's Children). Derrick was doing his best to stop crying, and Teresa was doing her best to comfort him with an arm around his shoulder, shushing him, and telling him that everything would be all right. Obviously, as far as Derrick was concerned, everything was definitely *not* all right.

"What's the matter, Derrick?" Mr. Usher asked, looking quite concerned. Derrick was not the sort of boy to get into a fight or to cry unless something was very wrong. Mr. Usher squatted down to look into the boy's eyes, which were red and swollen (as eyes get when one is crying, especially in the cold and wind). Teresa kept her arm around Derrick's shoulder.

At first Derrick did not want to say anything, but Teresa hugged him a little tighter and told him to tell Mr. Usher what had happened because Mr. Usher was nice and wouldn't be mad at him.

Derrick still cried and sniffled a bit. "Teresa and I were working in the office, helping Ms. Place put supplies away, just like you asked us to. We weren't doing anything wrong and were trying to be quiet and not disturb Principal Button. I was putting a box of new scissors up on a high shelf, and by accident the box fell and made a big noise, and Mr. Button came running into the room and shouted at me and told me I was being a nuisance and to go away! I was just trying to help and it was an accident!"

Mr. Usher looked at Teresa, and she quietly nodded at him as if to say, yes, that's pretty much just what happened.

"Well," Mr. Usher said slowly, "this is all most unusual. You're both very helpful in the office, and I know for a fact that Ms. Place and Mr. Button are more than happy to have you work there from time to time. I'll look into all of this, I can promise, and we'll find out what happened and why. But now, Derrick, dry your eyes and go back into class, and we'll talk more about this later." And with that, the Children and Mr. Usher stepped back through the door from the windy corridor into the warmth of their classroom.

The next day, as the Children were filing back into the classroom after lunch, noisily finding their way back to their seats, Mr. Usher quietly took Derrick aside and squatted down in front of him.

"Do you remember your problem in the office yesterday?" Mr. Usher asked. Derrick nodded. "Well," said Mr. Usher, "I've looked into it, and I think I know what happened and why. But I'd rather you understand how this sort of problem happens instead of just fixing it up and forgetting about it. So between you and me, the lessons we're going to work on in class for the next day or so may be especially interesting to you." And with that, Mr. Usher gave Derrick a little smiling wink and went up to the front of the class, leaving Derrick rather more confused than he had been before.

"Please get your coats and jackets on," Mr. Usher said to the Children. "We're going outside for a little project. Everyone bring paper and pencil and something to write on, and someone grab the tape measure and a ball of string from the tool box."

So the Children put on their coats and jackets, which they had just taken off a few minutes earlier. Some grumbled and asked each other why Mr. Usher hadn't just told them to stay outside in the first place, but most of the Children knew by now that Mr. Usher almost always did strange things for a very good reason. Soon they were all gathered out in the small woods behind the schoolyard, where thin willows and young oak trees grew and shed their leaves, and so many birds filled the air in spring time that you could hear them all the way over to the classrooms. In autumn, the dark, damp ground was covered with leaves and twigs that crunched and rustled underfoot.

Mr. Usher asked the Children to measure off a square on the ground that measured six feet on a side and to mark the square with the string they had found in the toolbox. When the yellow string was measured out and stretched on the ground, and two of the Children had wisely put large stones on the string to keep it in place, Mr. Usher asked the Children to sit around the square on the ground.

"Now, Children," Mr. Usher began, "we're going to learn a very important skill today, more important than how to throw a baseball or how to make peanut butter sandwiches, and almost as important as how to read or write or do addition and subtraction. I want you to look at the square we've marked out, and I want you to write down everything that's in the square, or is happening in the square, or is part of the square, or makes something happen in the square. Everything. Work together and come up with a list. Tell me when you're finished." And with that, Mr. Usher sat down with his back to a thick young oak tree, pulled his hat down over his eyes, and looked as if he had decided to take a little nap.

The Children looked and wrote and talked and discussed, and soon they had long lists of everything in the square. They all had noticed the obvious things you would think would be in a square of forest ground, like leaves and twigs and bugs and bushes and dirt. They dug down under the soil and found worms and ants and more bugs, and even an old dirty shoe. After a good long while, the Children all called to Mr. Usher that they had completed their lists. Mr. Usher tilted his hat back (I don't think he was ever asleep at all) and came back over to where the Children all bustled together to show him what each of them had written. Mr. Usher took out a big piece of paper from under his overcoat, unfolded it, drew a big square, and began to write down all of the things that the Children called out to him. Soon the square on the paper was nearly filled, and the Children sat back, looking very pleased with themselves because they had written down everything they could see in this piece of the forest.

"You've certainly seen quite a bit in that square," said Mr. Usher thoughtfully. "It's a very busy square for being such a small piece of ground out here in a little part of the forest, isn't it? But I think there may be a few items you've missed."

Some of the Children began to argue and say that no, they were sure they had found all of the things in the square, but the other Children shushed them, knowing that Mr. Usher could usually see things in ways that other people couldn't.

"How did all of these plants grow here?" Mr. Usher asked. "Surely, plants don't grow in the dark. There must be sunlight in that square, but no one has mentioned it."

"But the sun isn't in the square; it's way up there in the sky," said Kara. "You said to make a list of things that were in the square or happening in the square."

"The sun may be up in the sky," said Mr. Usher, "but the light it sheds down on earth most certainly hits this spot of the forest. And with the light comes warmth. We can't *see* warmth, but if it weren't there, then this square of the forest would be a very cold place. So sunlight is a very important part of the square, even if the sun itself is outside the square."

The Children all nodded their heads and agreed that sunlight should definitely go on to their lists.

"And what *is* that odor I smell?" Mr. Usher asked, bending down very low, so low in fact that his nose nearly touched the leaves and dark soil where the Children had dug up the square. "I don't know what the smell is, but it's in the square and therefore must be part of what we're looking at. Perhaps it's because the ground is moist, which it is, even though no one put 'moist' or 'wet' or 'water' on their list. I think moist soil is very different from dry soil. Wouldn't you agree?"

Some of the Children nodded their heads in agreement, but other of the Children wrinkled their brows and thought hard, and weren't at all sure that things which they couldn't even see should be on the list of things in the square.

Mr. Usher stood up and stepped into the middle of the square and motioned for all of the Children to do the same. Soon they were all standing inside the yellow string, crowded tightly shoulder to shoulder. Mr. Usher asked all of the Children to be quiet and then he asked, "What *is it* that I feel?" All of the Children stood very still, listening now and smelling and trying to feel what Mr. Usher was feeling, but the only thing they could feel was the cool autumn breeze blowing gently through the trees. Finally, Derrick shouted out "Wind! You're feeling the air move!" and Mr. Usher clapped him on the back and gave him a big smile.

"Quite right, Derrick," said Mr. Usher. "There's air above the square, and it's not always the same air. It moves in and moves away so that the air that's here right now won't be the air that's here when I'm finished speaking. And the forest animals come and go like the wind, here one minute and gone the next—like the squirrels that run about and maybe drop an acorn in the square, then run away. They're part of the square, even if we don't see them right this minute. Think hard, now. Is there something else that's part of the square that wasn't here before and may go away again? Something that's here right now, just this afternoon, a very important part of the square?"

The Children looked around as hard as they could, smelling the air and feeling the breeze, and straining the ears to listen, but they couldn't see anything new. Then, after a minute, one child shouted out the answer, and probably you have already figured it out.

"Us!" shouted Aaron. "We're in the square and didn't even realize it!" All of the Children laughed at themselves for being so silly and missing such an obvious riddle, and Mr. Usher wrote a big "US" in the middle of the square on his paper. Then he folded the paper back up into his pocket and started back towards the schoolyard.

"Come on, back to the room," he said. "It's getting chilly here, and I think our work in the forest is done for now. We'll go back inside where it's warm and try to figure out just what we have learned."

When the Children were all back in the classroom and had once again taken off their coats and jackets and hung them up with their scarves on the hooks along the back wall, Mr. Usher asked them to gather 'round and listen carefully as he had something important to discuss. As you have heard before, whenever Mr. Usher asked the Children to gather 'round, they knew that they might be in for a treat or a surprise, or at the very least they would learn about something that would prove useful to remember. So they pushed their chairs into a half circle around Mr. Usher and soon were quiet and ready to listen.

"Today, we took the first step in understanding what a system is," began Mr. Usher. "We can think of a system as any place or thing that has different parts to it. In class, we spend a lot of time asking questions and finding problems to answer. We can think of a system as a place where we find questions and answers that are all somehow connected to one another. Simple systems have only a few parts and are easy to look at and understand. Complicated systems have lots of parts and are hard to understand, or maybe even impossible to understand."

Some of the Children looked at each other with worried faces because they weren't happy to hear that there might be things that were so difficult that it was impossible for even Mr. Usher to understand them.

"Out in the forest we looked at a system, and we tried to learn something about it. The system we studied was a piece of ground marked out by the yellow string. We found as many parts as we could and made a list of them. Now, Children, do you think we saw every single thing in that area, or did we maybe miss some?"

The Children talked amongst themselves for a minute and then Schuyler said, "I think we listed everything. If there'd been anything else, we would have seen or felt or smelled it."

"What about the size of the system itself?" Mr. Usher asked. "We felt the air blowing through the square as breeze and put that on the list since it seemed important, even though the air was coming from somewhere way outside the square. But we didn't decide how deep the system might go below the ground, and we didn't decide how high up into the sky it might go. Does anyone have any suggestions about how big the system we studied really is?" The Children looked very puzzled and confused, and no one raised his or her hand.

"And what about things that we can't see or feel or taste or smell or hear? When we stepped into the square, when we were part of the system, did we bring happiness or sadness or friendship or love or hatred into the system along with us? Are those things part of a system?"

Schuyler raised his hand and Mr. Usher called on him. "Mr. Usher, you're just asking questions, not giving us answers about this system. Can we really answer these questions or are systems just too hard for us to understand?"

Mr. Usher chuckled a little and said, "You've made a very good point, Schuyler. The most important thing about understanding a system is that the more questions you can ask about it, the more you will know in the end. And that's because you can decide to make the system almost anything you want it to be! You get to decide when to stop asking questions and concentrate on answering instead. But don't get discouraged. Think how much we learned about our system in the forest! We learned about all of the plants and bugs and soil that are in that part of the forest, and we learned that some things stay in the system for a long time, like the dirt and the old tennis shoe, and that some things stay in the system for only a very short time, like the breeze."

"Or like us!" chimed in several students, and Mr. Usher laughed and said, "Yes, just like us."

Michael had been staring thoughtfully out the window during most of the time Mr. Usher had been talking, and now he raised his hand. Mr. Usher called on him, and Michael screwed up his face in as hard-thinking a look as he could manage and said, "Mr. Usher, there's something I don't understand. If the breeze was part of the system, and we were part of the system while we were in the square, aren't we part of the system when we aren't in the square also? Isn't the breeze part of the system even before it gets to the square? What if the breeze carried some plant seeds with it from some other part of the forest and dropped the seeds in the square? Or what if one of us left behind a piece of litter or stepped on a little plant and killed it by accident? Even after we left, the litter would still be there, or the plants we stepped on would die. Doesn't that mean that things that are outside the square are really part of the system, too?

While Michael had been talking, Mr. Usher's smile grew bigger and bigger until he was grinning ear to ear. The Children knew that look on Mr. Usher's face meant that one of them had just said something or learned something that was very important, because learning something very important always made Mr. Usher happy enough to dance a jig.

"You're exactly right, Michael," Mr. Usher said, still smiling, and he gave Michael a big thumbs-up sign. "The more we look at systems, and the more questions we ask, the more we see that there's no such system as just a square on the ground in the forest. Things that happen in one place make things happen in other places. The little square we marked off in the forest is really part of a big system that might reach from below the ground up to the sun, and to faraway parts of the world. We need to remember that when we try to figure out how things work in a system, and most important, *why* they work the way they do. Because, Children, we should always be more interested in *why* something is than we are in knowing *what* something is. Tomorrow, we're going to look at a completely different sort of system, and we're going to ask *why* a lot more than we're going to ask *what*."

And with that, Mr. Usher asked the Children to push their chairs back into place and take out some books to read, which they did, though many of the Children were still trying to figure out whether air from the other side of the world should *really* be part of the system of their little square of forest ground.

And Derrick (who, you will remember, had been yelled at in the office) was probably the most confused of all. He'd been waiting patiently for Mr. Usher to tell him how *any* of this business about bugs and breezes and squares of yellow string in the forest had *anything* to do whatsoever with why the principal had shouted at him. As the Children took out their books and started to read, Mr. Usher came over to Derrick's desk, bent down low, and whispered in Derrick's ear: "Tomorrow we're going to study a new system, and I think we'll find out *why* the principal yelled at you." And with that, Mr. Usher gave Derrick a friendly smile, turned, and walked back to his big desk at the front of the class.

*   *   *   *

The Lesson of the Principal

The next morning, just after the Children had finished their quiet morning reading time, Mr. Usher asked them once more to gather 'round by the door and to form small groups of three or four students per group. When they were all in their groups, Mr. Usher held up his hand and the Children grew quiet.

"As I promised, today we're going to study a very different kind of system. This system doesn't have a lot of dirt and animals and bushes and the sort of things that we usually find out in nature, but it's a system all the same, and we want to learn all about how it works. *This* system is mostly made up of people and desks and cabinets full of tools that help us learn. We're going to study the system of the school office. I suggest you find a corner where your small group can sit down and watch, and write down all the parts of the System you see. Ready? Let's go!"

So Mr. Usher and the Children walked down the outside hall to the school office and went inside where Ms. Place was busy typing out worksheets and a student from another class was putting stacks of new paper away in the cabinets. Through a door the Children could see Principal Button talking on the telephone, and through another door they saw the nurse, Mr. Cross, sitting quietly on the nurse's couch with a student who was not feeling well.

The Children gathered in their small groups and found corners out of the way and began to watch and listen and write down all of the parts of the system that they could. And what a different system from the square of forest! Here, there were people and telephones and typewriters. There were stacks of paper and pencils and cabinets full of everything one uses in a classroom. There were electric lights and sinks and faucets, which meant that electricity and water must come from somewhere else, so they must be a part of the system as well. Sometimes new people would come into the office to get something from Ms. Place or to ask a question, and each time they would look around at all of the Children sitting here and there in the corners and wonder why the Children were so busy writing down odds and ends about a silly old office. (And, of course, by now you know without me telling you that every time someone new would come into the office, even if just for a minute, the Children would add that person to their system list, too.)

It was all of this "in and out" and "to and fro" of people and telephone calls that finally gave Derrick his idea. He whispered something to the other two Children in his group and quietly went up to Ms. Place, who was putting letters into a file folder behind her desk.

"Excuse me, Ms. Place," Derrick said. "May I ask you a question?"

"Of course you can, Derrick," replied Ms. Place, who liked Derrick quite a lot because he was so helpful when he came to work in the office. "I'm afraid I don't know what you're doing exactly, but if I can help, just ask."

"It's about the other day when I was working here and dropped the box of scissors on the floor and Principal Button yelled at me," said Derrick quietly. "I've thought and thought, and I can't understand why Principal Button would yell at me for dropping some scissors. I think maybe something else happened that I didn't see, and that's really why he was mad. Do you know if anything happened that day to make him mad?"

Ms. Place smiled at Derrick with a sad sort of smile because she remembered very well when Principal Button had yelled at him. "Well, dear, sometimes things do happen that make us upset or angry, and it can ruin a whole day. It can turn the nicest person into a grump, can't it? The day Principal Button yelled at you was a difficult day around this office, I can tell you! Early in the morning he got several telephone calls, and he was in a bad mood after that, but if you want to know more, you're going to have to ask him yourself."

About this time, Mr. Usher came up to Derrick and Ms. Place and knelt down beside Derrick. Derrick looked Mr. Usher in the eye, and he looked right back. "You know why he yelled at me, don't you?" Derrick asked.

Mr. Usher nodded. "Yes, I talked to him the next day. I did a little system study of my own, and it soon led me to the root of the problem, just as it has led you. Now if you want to know the answer to your question *why* did Principal Button yell at you, go on in and ask him. Don't worry, he's expecting you." And with a wink and a helpful pat on the shoulder, Mr. Usher stood up and walked over to another group of students.

Derrick took a big deep breath. Talking to the Principal was not something one usually did for fun, and he was more than a little afraid. But Derrick screwed up his courage and went over and knocked on Principal Button's half-open door.

Principal Button looked up from behind his desk, peering over the top of the old half-glasses that perched on the end of his nose. He waved Derrick over to the big chair in front of the desk, and Derrick sat down on the edge. This was the chair that you sat in if you were in trouble and had to go see the Principal, which made Derrick screw up his courage a little more yet.

Principal Button took off his glasses and ran his hand through his thick head of wavy grey hair. He leaned back in his tall black chair. "Derrick, I owe you an apology," he said. "I yelled at you the other day, and I didn't even know it until Mr. Usher came in here and told me that I'd upset you. I'm sorry. It wasn't your fault."

"If you don't mind my asking, why *did* you yell at me when I dropped the box of scissors?" Derrick asked. "Mr. Usher says we should try to understand why things happen, especially if it's something unusual, and getting yelled at for dropping scissors seems unusual."

"You're absolutely right, Derrick," Mr. Button replied. "I'll tell you. I was just in a dreadful mood that day. My car broke down in the morning, and I had to walk a mile in that nasty cold wind, not to mention that I stepped into a puddle of rain water and soaked my shoe right through. Then as soon as I got here to the office, my wife called and told me that our puppy had dug up the sprinklers again, and she had to call the yard man to come out and fix them because water was spraying everywhere. I love that dog, but you know how difficult puppies can be! And then on top of that I had a parent call me on the phone to say he was not at all happy with the grade his daughter had received on some test, and he got very angry about it. So I just got into the wrong mood, and wanted nothing more than peace and quiet for the rest of the day, when *wham* goes this loud sound, and I just yelled out at you. It wasn't your fault at all. You're a good boy, and we like having you help out in the office. I would have apologized earlier, except Mr. Usher came in with that twinkle in his eye and said he wanted to make a big lesson out of this, and I guess he has!"

Derrick felt like a big weight had lifted off of his shoulders. He thanked Principal Button and went back out into the main office just as Mr. Usher was gathering the rest of the Children together to return to the classroom. Mr. Usher gave Derrick a smile and winked over the heads of the other Children, and they all went together back down the outside hall.

When all of the Children were back again at their desks, Mr. Usher pulled another big piece of paper out of his desk and asked the Children to tell him all of the parts of the system that they had noted from the office. By now the Children had become quite good at this system game, and their lists were even longer than from the day before in the forest. They filled Mr. Usher's big paper with all of the parts and people they had seen in the office. They listed things that were always in the office like desks and the floor. They listed things that were sometimes in the office like Ms. Place and a cricket which had jumped in through an open window. They even listed things that were never in the office at all but must be a part of the system, like the people who sold paper to the school, and the parents who sent their Children to school every day.

When the big piece of paper was completely full of the Children's lists, Mr. Usher stopped writing and took his glasses off his nose to wipe them. He settled his glasses back on and faced the Children.

"You have all become nearly expert at this game I call Studying the System. Why, I'll bet that most grown-ups can't see all the things you can! You see, learning is all about understanding. When we want to understand something, we usually first ask *what* is there. After we know something about the *whats*, we can start asking about the *whys* and *hows*. And when we put all of those pieces together, then we've really learned something new.

"But the real reason we've spent almost two days with this game is that we need to know that studying and understanding are good not only in the classroom. We learned that out in the forest, didn't we? We also learned that when people are part of a system, their parts of the system are sometimes hardest of all to understand. Derrick found out that the reason Principal Button yelled at him the other day was because Mr. Button had a flat tire and two bad phone calls! Because Mr. Button was feeling bad that day, his feelings became part of the system, and Derrick learned that a system with Mr. Button feeling bad is not the same system as one with Mr. Button feeling cheery. Those are parts of the system that are very hard to find out, but sometimes they can be the most important part of all.

"Think about where and how you can use your new system studying skills. How about at home? People are a very important part of the Home System, aren't they? Maybe you want to understand why your father sets rules about bedtime, or why your mother seems always to take the side of your little brother, even when you think he's being a brat. Maybe it will help you see why you need to do your chores in the yard, or why we don't throw away old clothes if someone else can use them. There are all sorts of times at home when studying the system will help you understand things more clearly.

"Or what about out in the neighborhood, or on the playground? Sometimes things just don't make sense, like why one kid is bullying another, or why we have certain rules for certain games. Does your mother let you go over to some kids' houses and not to others'? Are there some roads you can cross and others you can't? Why? Probably there's a reason, and if you study the system of children and parents and houses and roads that makes up your neighborhood, I'll bet you'll find out the reasons before too long."

With that, Mr. Usher asked the Children to do some quiet reading until the end of the day, and he went up to his old wooden desk at the front of the class and sat down to correct some papers. After a while he looked out over the class and saw many of the Children gazing thoughtfully out the window, out at the schoolyard and the old oak tree, as if they were secretly writing lists in their heads of all the parts of the schoolyard system that they could see. Mr. Usher smiled to himself, and the smile grew even bigger when he looked over at Derrick, and for the first time in several days, Derrick *really* smiled back.

*　　　*　　　*　　　*

Before we check back in with Mr. Sun in the strangely shaped room full of chessboards and weather maps, we pause to reflect on the meat of what Mr. Usher and the Children have undertaken. We will break down the key steps of Understanding the System, and write a few postulates of our own, written in our shared language of *The Art of War*, to take back to Mr. Sun. Remember, this is the hard work of creating and using strategy, the stuff that takes time and resources, and sometimes leads to frustration and failure. All of those things are okay. If it were easy, there would be a cookbook recipe somewhere that we could follow. But that would be the recipe that someone else has already created for their own life trials, and we want the tools to create a recipe for our own trials, success, and happiness. Hang in there and before you know it, we will have created a list of tools that will help you understand the systems that surround your own pursuits of happiness.

Tangibles

The easiest systems to understand are those that are largely composed of tangible parts. Keeping in mind our discussion of subjectivity and objectivity, if we assume that the physical world is real, and therefore quantifiable, we can objectively measure many of the components of a purely physical system.

In the era of Einsteinian physics, we believe that everything in the physical realm is made up of energy and/or matter. If the system we are studying is a Petri dish full of bacteria, the components are relatively few. "Matter" will consist of the dish, the culturing gel, the bacteria, and, should we wish to extend our concept of this system, perhaps the oven that the dish is in, and the lab building which houses the oven. "Energy" may include the warmth from the oven, the electricity that fuels the oven, and the rather lesser amount of bio-energy radiated by the bacteria as they consume the gel and grow.

Each of these components has a flux, or flow, through the system. Energy flows into the system through electrical wires, heating elements, and the food energy stored in the auger gel. Energy flows out of the system as radiated heat through the walls of the culturing oven and through the energy radiated from the bacteria themselves. Matter flows into the system from us as we add the elements to the Petri dish, and matter flows out of the system when we remove the elements at the end of the culturing period. The growth of bacteria over time represents the conversion of energy to matter within the system, and the reverse is true as the bacteria die and decay.

Therefore, given a narrow concept of what is included in the system and what is not, energy and matter flux are measurable. Once we widen our view of what constitutes the system, as Mr. Usher's Children learned in the forest, the complexity of possible relationships grows rather quickly. But we should always take the easiest steps first.

Our first postulate therefore is: count the bushels of rice and the spears in their racks.

Intangibles

Many systems contain components that are non-physical. Often these components are the relationships between physical parts of the system. They can include such strong but subjective forces as love, hate, values, faith, judgment, loyalty, and desire. Recognizing that such a component resides in the system is a crucial step. Is it possible to do more, to measure or place a value on a value?

Many systems are, in fact, dominated by intangible components. A squad of soldiers hunkers down in their foxhole under attack by an unseen enemy. The foxhole is a system within the larger context of the battle, defined by those specific, non-interchangeable soldiers. A grenade lands in the foxhole. The entire future of the system depends on whether or not one or more soldiers, drawn by an intangible force, will fall on the grenade. The intangible bond, or lack thereof, among the soldiers is, in this instant, more important to our understanding of the system than are the soldiers themselves.

A colonial power spends decades or centuries solidifying its control over the life, economy, and culture of a far-off land. Its best diplomats spend careers studying and understanding the system of the colony in order to forecast change, adapt, and perpetuate rule. Along comes one little man, a Mohandas Gandhi, with a level of understanding and faith that is better adapted to the mid-twentieth century than that of the British Empire, and suddenly the colonial system that was the British Raj is turned upside down.

Two families pass through the volatile disputes and battles that describe life in the family unit. One family, despite their best efforts to understand their issues and problems, becomes dysfunctional and ends in divorce, and the children grow up to view parenting as an iffy proposition at best. The other family sorts out its differences, struggles through the years, and retains a mutual sense of affection that lasts a lifetime. The intangible components of each system have overridden the physical components in terms of importance.

Even if we cannot quantify the relative strength of these intangible forces, our recognition of their importance allows us to arrive at a more accurate model of the system under analysis. The recognition of intangible components of a system demands that we include them in the full light of our own self-realized understanding of subjectivity and objectivity. Concretely, then, our understanding of how any system works, from the most mundane Petri dish to the most complex interpersonal or abstract interactions, is based on our own observations, definitions, and impact on the system as we observe it.

Our second postulate therefore is: measure the courage of your soldiers, the faith of your people, and the stealth of your spies.

Gain and Loss

Once we identify as many relevant components of the system as possible, we can try to quantify, either on a relative or on an absolute scale, the gains and losses realized by each component during the period of observation.

Which components, both tangible and intangible, have grown, lengthened, become stronger or more dominant? Which components, both tangible and intangible, have grown smaller, shorter, weaker, less active, or less powerful? For tangible components, the measurements can be quantitative as we use analytical tools to weigh, measure, size, and scale what we can lay our hands on during the period of observation. For intangible components, we will have to be satisfied with a relative scale: is there more or less present now than when we started to observe? Has the relationship strengthened or weakened?

One important quality check of your understanding of the system is to do a zero sum equation. In the simplest system, one based on wholly tangible components, the inputs and outputs of the system, or the total sum of components over time, should balance. We look at the value of all the system components in an initial condition and compare these values to all of the system components under final conditions. If the total values balance, then the system satisfies the test for a zero sum equation, and we know we have investigated all of the possible components of the system. If they do not balance, then either we missed something, or there are intangible components that cannot be measured which contribute to the system.

Economists love the clarity of numbers. When analyzing a company, the balance sheet provides the fastest, surest test of whether or not the entire picture has been viewed. If the balance sheet doesn't balance, well of course the analysis is flawed. In studying physical systems, we rely on the paradigm that energy and matter are always conserved, and therefore it is easy to test for a zero sum result. In the simple matter of the Petri dish, were we able to quantify every bit of matter and energy within a certain boundary? Our knowledge of physics tells us that either a balance exists, or we have messed up somewhere.

Systems with intangible components are more difficult to balance. Since intangible components cannot be measured, they cannot form a portion of a true zero sum equation. Some systems will yield a zero sum if viewed narrowly, but will provide a non-zero sum result if viewed more broadly. A scientist for a private company is working in a laboratory. She mixes chemicals in a test tube, and since she is a good chemist and is careful in her work, she can account for all of the energy and matter that have both entered the test tube and that leave the test tube after the experiment is complete. The system within the test tube provides a zero sum result, with all components accounted for. However, the experiment is a breakthrough in chemical polymers; the company sells the patent for millions of dollars, and the annual profit and loss statement shows a huge increase in revenue. The economic system of the company, a broader system than the test tube, does not show a zero sum result, but a very positive result, largely based on what took place in the small test tube.

This strongly suggests that the occurrence of zero sum equations, the neatest and tidiest view of a system, is dependent on the size of the system that we choose to study. In a small system, it is easy to balance the flow of components. In a very large system, it is only our belief in quantum physics, the equality of matter and energy, which allows us to believe that we have accounted for all of the components. Most defined systems fall somewhere in between. There are gains and losses that we can't quantify, but that we believe exist, and that may be important.

Our third postulate therefore is: the enemy is not known by his portrait at one sitting, but by watching and studying him over time, by assessing his ebb and flow.

Boundaries

Mr. Usher and his Children faced a problem of infinite proportions when they poked around in the forest behind the school. Even the Children recognized the problem as they continued to ask questions about what they saw and whether or not it belonged in their system. How big is the system and what does it contain? Where are the boundaries of the system that we are studying? When and where do we stop? This is a critical point of judgment in system analysis; failure to set an appropriate boundary can lead to either an incomplete solution or an enormous waste of resources.

Let's go back to my classroom in the Philippines where some college students struggled with this problem, only to find it landing right back in their own laps in a very real way.

*   *   *   *

The farm college filled a sandy backwater, wedged between the coral sand beach and a wide swath of neatly pruned coconut groves. The simple concrete buildings had wooden shutters open to the mild sea breezes, and spotless red tile floors that the students kept polished with the split husks of brown coconuts. The Spartan classrooms held only old wooden desks, colorful calendars and travel posters faded from years of indirect sunlight, and a narrow chalkboard. Rich smells of decaying rice stalks and manure wafted through the classroom from the livestock pens, along with the contentious clucking of hungry chickens and the anxious grunts of pigs pushing about in the mud.

The students sat at their desks in orderly rows of white smiles, jet-black hair, brown skin, white shirts and blouses, and cleanly pressed pants and skirts. They smiled eagerly as I entered their room. The chattering quickly died down and changed from a musical mix of Tagalog, Visayan, and Spanish to English.

The topic of my guest lecture was deforestation. We sat in the perfect teaching laboratory for the subject. During the previous ten months, I had climbed steep volcanoes, dragged my way through the mist-shrouded rain forests, surveyed sunny sugarcane fields, and slogged through the lowland rice paddies that cover most of the island. My faculty hosts and I were studying the relationship of population to land use in a tropical setting of unparalleled fertility and irrepressible poverty.

Deforestation is an issue of evangelical emotion in the environmental community. Many prominent scientists believe it is the single greatest issue of our time, or should be, and I'm inclined to agree with them. The threats of global deforestation are equally as ominous as those of nuclear war. The great tropical rain forests, sources of a large percentage of the oxygen we breathe, are disappearing at a catastrophic rate. It was an emotional local issue as well. A single generation ago the parents of these students hid from Japanese bayonets and bullets in jungle so dense that a few meters of growth provided an impenetrable green wall. Now most of those same rugged hillsides and secretive valleys are as clear of trees as a Nebraska plain. A part of their heritage, culture, economy, and soul has vanished overnight.

First, I asked the students to explain deforestation to me. The answers were predictable and correct. The thick, steaming jungles that had once draped the nearby mountainsides had now receded far up the slopes and in many places disappeared altogether. The students witnessed deforestation every day, with far-off smoke plumes marking the day's toll of slash and burn.

I asked the students why the forests had been cut, and the answers were again predictable. The poor farmers, always in need of new and fresh land on which to grow food, cut the trees and farmed farther and farther up the slopes each year. The soil's fertility faded with each month of exposure to the wasting tropical sun. The farmers moved on and cut more trees, and the forests disappeared. Always more people, more children, and the beautiful forest, source of water, wood, animals, plants, beauty, and mystique, sacrificed to the inevitable march of time. If we can teach the peasants to use the forest resources, the students said, instead of destroying them, the problem will be solved.

I asked how many of them wanted to stop deforestation. They all raised their hands. I asked how many of them had ever been up to the rain forest, had hiked up the volcano, had talked to the farmers in the hills. A few raised their hands. I asked the students how many of them drank Coca-Cola or Pepsi or Fanta, and, puzzled, every one of them raised a hand. "Good," I said calmly.

"Now we have identified the real culprits of deforestation. It's all of you sitting in this room, in cooperation with big rich American corporations."

I had their full attention.

Like most people in the proud countries of the developing world, many Filipinos like Americans as individuals, but they don't particularly like America as a concept. I grew up rooting for the San Francisco Giants, and I'm sure I would have liked some of the Los Angeles Dodgers as neighbors, but the institution of the Dodgers was an abomination to me. I had just accused these fresh-faced students of being covert Dodger lackeys.

"Why do the farmers cut the trees?" I asked. Because they need to grow food, the students answered. "Why do they need to grow food on slopes so steep that sometimes they have to tie ropes to themselves to weed their crops?" I asked. Because no one owns that land up there, no one wants it, the students answered. "Why can't the farmers grow their food on the lower slopes, on the broad alluvial fans, and on the flat coastal land, in all of this bountiful, deep volcanic soil that stretches from the sea to the mountains, in soil so fertile that if you plant a nail it'll grow?" I asked. Because all of that area is used for growing other crops, they answered, as the beginning of worry crossed their faces. "What's the main crop that's grown on the good land?" I asked. Sugarcane. "What's the main ingredient in Coke and Pepsi and Fanta, besides water?" Sugar, they answered. "And where do you think all of the sugar comes from?" I asked. The students looked at each other; finally one raised her hand.

"If we stopped drinking so much American soda, the landowners wouldn't grow so much sugar, and the land could be used to grow more food. The rain forests would stop disappearing," she said, with a look of wonder and realization. "It's us. We're causing the forests to be cut."

All of the students stopped and looked out the window and up the mountain, and no one said anything for a minute. Some of the boys squared their shoulders and wanted to argue, but they didn't because they weren't sure at all who was "right." Guilt had just shifted from the farmers, way up on the mountain, into the classroom.

We spent the rest of the hour talking about all of the things that affect the forest, not just the easy and obvious ones. We sketched a far-reaching matrix on the old chalkboard showing distant relationships between farmers, landowners, producers, consumers, trees, animals, water, and everything else we could think of that is part of the real rain forest system. Of course, boycotting Coke would have a miniscule impact on their own rain forest, and by the end of the hour they knew it. The relationship of ecology to cash crops in the developing countries is hardly a problem that can be addressed in an hour. But they also understood that the easy and obvious answers are rarely the end of a question.

There are mega-thinking theorists who argue that the beating wings of a butterfly in Canada can affect the onset of a hurricane in the Caribbean. I don't know that we will ever address that possibility any more than we can map the direct causal relationship of soda consumption to worldwide deforestation. But I think that there are about thirty ex-agriculture students somewhere in the humid, rich islands of the southern Philippines who see the complex world of cause and effect more clearly every time they reach into the refrigerator.

*   *   *   *

It is arguable that there *are no* boundaries, that all systems and all components of all systems are inextricably linked to every other component and system in the physical universe. One could extend this argument to intangible components as well. Often, however, especially when the area of interest is other than philosophy, it is helpful, or maybe even essential, to set a boundary beyond which we do not consider the inputs and outflows, the influence of external entities, to be relevant to our study. *We* set the boundaries that we want to consider, just as we *de facto* set the way we observe the world around us due to the subjective nature of observation. One of the most important parts of studying anything is to set the boundary conditions. Only then can the answer be relevant, and only in terms of the pre-set boundary conditions. Given a different set of boundary conditions, surely the observable aspects of the system, the results of our inspection and analysis, would be different.

Consider again the chemist and the test tube. Within the boundary conditions described by the test tube, the chemist can perform carefully prepared experiments that will yield meaningful results. If the chemist is careful and strictly follows the guidelines each time the experiment is performed, the results will be repeatable, and new knowledge may be gained and accepted by others as more or less irrefutable. If the chemist chooses boundary conditions which are too broad, expanding the studied system to include not only the test tube, but also the laboratory, the building housing the laboratory, and the town in which the building stands, the conditions can never be repeated to the desired degree of accuracy. The results of the experiment in the test tube itself will be difficult to interpret at best and will likely be meaningless in the face of so many variables.

How different the task of the philosopher who considers the meaning of life! If the philosopher sets narrow boundary conditions, looking only at tangible components of a tightly defined control group, he risks missing the over-arching relationships, passions, and forces that affect his system. It means little to state that a careful analysis of the theology of three individuals, on a particular day, in a particular setting, with carefully controlled temperature, pressure, and humidity, tends to monotheism.

Our fourth postulate therefore is: the good warrior knows the borders of his enemy and does not chase diversions beyond the frontier of his own choosing.

Lumpers and Splitters

In the Falconer seminar, I used a very simple elementary school-level tool to demonstrate how differently we can each quantify the world around us. On the table I emptied the contents of a worn brown paper bag. The pile consisted of coins and paper money from dozens of countries, several partial sheets of stamps, a couple of old credit cards, a folded packet of traveler's checks, an ATM card, and a torn sheet of lined paper upon which had been scrawled in black ink "IOU $5.25, Jan. 24, 1978. Jim." I asked my students to study the contents of the table and organize them into meaningful groups.

There are a large number of ways to sort out these items. A few possibilities might be sorting by

Place of origin
Type of tender
Composition (paper, metal, plastic)
Age
Face value
Market value
Size
Weight

With a little thought, even Mr. Usher's Children would come up with a very long list of additional possible groupings, each as valid as any other, depending on how you want to study the system labeled "the pile of things on the table."

There are two kinds of people in the world: lumpers and splitters. Lumpers like to generalize, stand back, and see the big picture. A lumper will look at the table and put all of the items into the category "legal tender," or maybe in two or three sub-categories. Where the lumpers see similarities, splitters like to break things down, sort them out, and find the areas of difference. A splitter will look at the table and find as many categories as there are items to be sorted, or more.

Lumpers and splitters see the world very differently. Since the nature of the observer is critical to how the universe around us appears, we need to know where on this continuum we, or our fellow observers, fit.

Paleontology is the study of fossils and how they have changed over the span of geologic time. Paleontologists try to identify discreet changes in the evolution of a set of fossils, and through this identification they can correlate species and time.

When does a wolf become a dog, or a German Sheppard become a golden retriever, and how can you tell from looking only at the bones? A lumper will look at the disparate sets of bones and say, "all are canines." The splitter will find some difference in the skeletons, be it length or weight or bone density, or some angular disparity in how the parts fit together and say, "We have different beasts here. These represent different species."

Who is right? Both are, as long as one admits his or her bias and allows the other to admit of his or hers.

Let's think about a study of grass, which is easy for anyone to do; just take your class outside. It is almost inconceivable that we would, for any reason, be interested in the exact characteristics of individual blades of grass in a backyard lawn, despite the fact that they are all, undeniably, unique. It is more likely that, should we be interested in grass, we want to look at the similarities and differences of grass in various parts of the lawn, or on different lawns, or in wild and domestic habitats, under a variety of conditions. Therefore, we might need to lump many blades of grass into a single category by species or location or another variable.

Let us think, on the other hand, that we are studying a system with as many individual components as there are blades of grass on our back lawn. We own a feedlot, and we want to understand the way our cows grow. We could lump all of the cows as "cows," but we would acquire little data that could be sorted and analyzed to tell us anything meaningful. We might, in this case, be forced to treat each cow as a unique part of the system, splitting out many different categories for analysis. Or, if we were short on resources, we could take a random sample of all of the cows, extrapolating the results over the entire population of the feedlot. The first approach would be more accurate, as we have split the group as finitely as possible and collected a large number of observations. The second approach may be less accurate, but it would save time and resources and may be adequate for our needs.

In selecting how to organize the system for study, we make both conscious and unconscious decisions about what is important to us and what is not. Does the relative size or strength or amount of something determine its importance to the system? Can we ignore the small, weak, or under-represented?

We are studying a plot of land and find a toxic chemical concentrated in parts per *billion*. There's not much but enough to get our attention in a hurry because this is a highly toxic chemical. A very small radiation leak in a large nuclear power plant is a highly significant event. Harry Truman, a small, poorly publicized compromise of a vice president, was overlooked by just about everyone … until he dropped a couple of bombs, saved Berlin, and reconstructed the international political face of the twentieth century. Small, dynamic parts of the system cannot be overlooked.

What about the obverse? Asked to analyze and understand a beaker of water, a chemist will test for organic and inorganic compounds to look for what the water contains. But what about the water itself? In all likelihood, more than 99% of what is in the beaker is just plain water, but the chemist will ignore all of those boring triplets of two hydrogens and an oxygen. Something that is more or less a constant in the system may often be overlooked, just because it is so dominant, so pervasive.

There are times we want to see the forest and times we need to see the trees.

Who decides what to look at and what to ignore, where to spend time and energy and where to bypass, what is small but terribly relevant, and what is large but passé? Who makes all of these choices? You do. And no one can tell you that you're wrong. Misguided maybe, but not wrong.

Our fifth postulate for understanding the System is: to know the whole, the warrior must know its parts; to know the parts, the warrior must organize them. To organize the parts, the warrior must know his or her goal, or she/he is merely shuffling pieces on the board.

Relationships: One-way, Bilateral, and Multilateral

Isaac Newton, having been bonked on the head by an apple, extrapolated that between any two physical bodies there exists a force of gravitational attraction that is proportional to the mass of the two bodies and inversely proportional to the distance between them. There are an infinite number of similar relationships that help describe the systems around us. These are the webs of relationships that exist between the individual tangible and intangible components of any system that we observe.

Let us view a simple food chain through the eyes of a lumper. The chain has four individual components: energy (the sun), producers (plants), consumers (animals), and decomposers (beasties in the ground). There is a relationship between each of these groups and at least one other group. Plants use sun energy to grow. Animals eat plants to grow. Animals defecate and die, to be eaten by decomposers, which release nutrients back to the soil to help plants grow. There are a lot of other factors at work, but for a lumper, that's all we need to know.

The relationships in such a simple chain are one-way relationships, at least through one pass of the cycle. Plants grow under the influence of sunlight, but the sun is not affected one bit by the plants' growth. Animals benefit from eating the plants, but the individual plant that is eaten derives nothing in return. (Of course the plant's offspring may well benefit from the cycling of nutrients, but we are looking now at individual plants and animals only.) Decomposers benefit from the waste and carcasses that fall nearby, but surely the deceased animals that provide the feast couldn't care less at that point. These are truly one-way relationships.

Bilateral relationships are only slightly more complicated. Again, referring to our elementary school biology class, we recall the example of symbiosis between a flower and a bee. The bee pollinates the flower, and the flower provides food for the hive.

During the years of the Cold War, the world operated under the heavy shadow of a strong bilateral political system. In one corner were the United States and the NATO countries, and in the other corner the USSR and the Warsaw Pact nations. Despite a yearning for neutrality, most other countries were dragged politically, economically, and socially into and out of one of the two camps. Some countries managed to stay perched on the sidelines, but from a sufficiently distant viewpoint, the important international questions from 1950–1985 were bilateral in nature. Certainly the citizens of Vietnam, Angola, Afghanistan, and most of Central America and the Middle East would agree.

In the post-Cold War era, relationships among nations have grown far more multilateral. The groupings that we choose, whether we look at them as lumpers or splitters, and via the language of economics, social construction, religion, politics, wars, or any number of other choices, do not comprise largely two camps, but a more fluid, changing, and tangled web. There is no question that the current geopolitical environment is far more complex than it was in 1960.

A "web" of course is the perfect symbol for depicting the range of relationships among multiple components of many real systems. The chain we described earlier is comprised of relatively simple one-way relationships: small animals eat plants, big animals eat small animals, big animals die and are eaten by beasties. In the real world, one in which we back off from the security of being perfect lumpers, there exists a complicated web of food production, consumption, decomposition, and recycling of both matter and energy. Describing all of the multilateral relationships that exist among organic components, even within a square meter of a backyard system, is as difficult and complex as describing all of the geopolitical relationships in the world.

Relationships, whether they are tangible or intangible, are the glue that holds a system together, and the system cannot be understood, even to a first order of precision, if just the components are mapped and the relationships between them are ignored.

Our sixth postulate therefore is: to fully understand the forest of trees and the braiding of streams, the warrior must understand the forces that bind the one to the other.

Possibility vs. Probability

As with lumpers and splitters, there are two kinds of people in the world: those who do not believe something is possible until it is proven, and those who believe anything is possible, no matter how improbable. The former are generally scientists, and the latter philosophers. Someone who shares a bit of both points of view is wise.

In considering what to include and what to ignore when looking at a system, we have to make decisions about what is probable and what is possible, and which of these categories is relevant to us. Mr. Usher's Children discussed the philosophical problem regarding the existence of the table (and as I mentioned before, this is an easy and *really* fun exercise to conduct in any class or training room). The pure scientist, dealing with the objective reality of the table says that the table certainly is "there." If one is studying the system of the living room, it is not necessary to consider the case where the table does not really exist because empirically it does. The philosopher will challenge this assumption, citing our discussion of Bell's Theorem, and state with equal promise that the table is only part of the living room system because the observer makes it so. He puts more weight on the possibility that the table may not exist, and less on the probability that it does.

This issue becomes more important when we look to the future instead of concentrating on the present. Electricity existed before Ben Franklin put his key onto a kite and before Thomas Edison hooked a bulb to a wire. It existed in either a natural state (lightning) or in a future state waiting to be discovered or invented. Why, then, should not a good scientist say, when queried about the table, "there is an equal probability that the table exists and does not exist, but I don't know how to deal with the latter, therefore I will not consider it at this time"?

The wider we open the system to what is possible, taking into account the future, the more potential opportunities, the greater number of possible solutions to questions and problems will arise. If you are seeking a quick answer to a well-constrained problem, you may choose to discard wider factors with lower probabilities. If you are stuck, if the answers you seek are not obvious at all, looking at the improbable may be the best choice. Remember, electricity, vaccines, nuclear weapons, steam engines, cell phones, the printed word, and the longbow were all impossible, once upon a time.

Our seventh postulate is: a good general knows that the impossible is probably just improbable.

Reframing Answers

Having made a series of conscious decisions regarding how we want to view, construct, and understand our system, the answers, observations, and conclusions that we draw must be qualified, either implicitly or explicitly. The qualifiers "from my point of view," "given the boundary conditions," "with a high degree of probability," and others should be part of framing conclusions and answers. Often we take these qualifiers as implied. Unfortunately, over time the conclusions to one problem become the foundation for another set of challenges, and the qualifiers are lost. We fail to understand the limits to which conclusions may rightly be applied, and then the logical piers of our thought may be built on sand instead of rock. To complete the quality control loop of our logical progression, we must revisit the assumptions upon which past conclusions are based to test for any apparent weaknesses.

This is the place for honesty, to tell the world that no, we don't have the answer in its absolute. Our findings are qualified by the limitations of our own observation. We may make less on the lecture circuit, but our honesty is preserved and the qualifying statements remind and prompt those who come behind to question before they accept. The next question may be "Well, what if I changed this or that condition or this or that assumption? Would the result be the same or different?" Immediately, by qualifying the statement, we have set in place a new set of possible questions that may further validate a clear understanding of the question at hand.

Our eighth postulate is: absolute honesty requires the warrior to be more honest and less absolute.

Communicating Results

How do we capture multiple components and complex relationships in a way that is meaningful to both ourselves and to anyone else? If our observed system is simple, a written description or a mathematical formula uses languages that are shared by a wide range of audiences. In high school chemistry class, we learn that the system of a test tube, water, and salt, can be described simply as

$$NaCl \text{ (in the presence of water)} = Na^+ + Cl^-.$$

We understand that, in all cases (or at least all of those that concern us as we strive to get a decent grade in chemistry class), table salt (sodium chloride), when placed in water, dissolves into two ions, a positive sodium ion and a negative chloride ion.

In both formulaic and English languages, we have just presented our understanding of the test tube system of water and salt. Anyone with the most basic knowledge of either chemistry or English can understand how we view this system.

Most systems are more complex than this simple test tube. Most issues, challenges, and problems that we try to study and understand have multiple components with complex webs of relationships, both tangible and intangible. How do we efficiently and effectively describe the system of "my family," the system of "my company," the system of "job opportunities," or the system of "my faith"?

Visual aids are perhaps the best way to communicate complex systems relationships. Maps portray geographical systems; family trees illustrate complex ancestral relationships; organizational charts are snapshots of corporate authority. Use these concepts to portray your vision in a manner that others can share.

In our high school seminar, I only required one deliverable from my students during the semester. I asked that each student select a system, analyze it according to the several criteria we had discussed, and then present their findings to the group. The presentation could take no more than ten minutes, and the goal was to impart a full and complete understanding of the studied system to the audience in that time. Visual aids were strongly encouraged, though the nature of those aids was left totally to the presenter. The results were astonishing, and in many cases solidified my growing sense that these kids were a lot smarter than I.

One student used a series of cardboard tubes and mirrors to demonstrate his conceptualization of the system "My Psyche." Another mixed the ingredients for some chocolate chip cookies to relay her analysis of "The Brain." A third used a family tree-type of flow chart to illustrate the system "Surfers and Surfing Conflicts Off Point Loma." Another used an array of colored inks and pen weights in a complex matrix to describe not only the ancestral but also interpersonal relationships of an extended family. Each had just ten minutes to impart their vision to a group of their peers, and without these uniquely creative props, they would have failed. Creative communication resulted in memorable success.

Our final postulate on systems analysis therefore is: the general who shares his vision may find himself at the head of a large army; the general who keeps his vision to himself will likely fight alone.

*   *   *   *

Whew. We finally find ourselves back in the strange triangular room with Mr. Sun, who is furiously typing at a computer keyboard with one hand, dialing a phone with the other, and watching game film of the Packers and the 49ers on a big screen. He seems very busy, so we watch quietly from the corner. After a while, he notices us and laughs apologetically.

"Sorry to keep you waiting," he says, hanging up the phone and pausing the game film. "But it looks like you are writing a few new postulates for my sequel. I get wrapped up in my work; understanding complex systems is difficult work that takes a lot of time. The problem is that if you don't put in the time and concentration you frequently miss something really important, and then all the problem solving that follows is based on bad data. In fact, I think this is the most common source of really serious errors of judgment and bad strategy. Some people call this 'garbage in, garbage out,' and they are right. Look at this football film for instance," he says, switching the big screen into action again. "The Packers could work from sun up to sun down all season long, but if one cornerback fails to anticipate the crossing pattern when they blitz, so much for the Super Bowl."

Mr. Sun hits a few keystrokes, and the game film disappears, replaced by passages from *The Art of War* on three screens.

"In a world where we have proven that truly objective data are rare, the more we can understand the factual components of the problem, the better our proposed solutions will be. That's why I spent so much time in my book on the importance of knowledge. Take a look and let's see if we agree with these interpretations."

Sun Tzu says: *Whether the object be to crush an army, to storm a city, or to assassinate an individual, it is always necessary to begin by finding out the names of the attendants, the aides-de-camp, and door-keepers and sentries of the general in command.*

Sun Tzu says: *The natural formation of the country is the soldier's best ally; but a power of estimating the adversary, of controlling the forces of victory, and of shrewdly calculating difficulties, dangers and distances, constitutes the test of a great general. He who knows these things will win his battles. He who knows them not will surely be defeated.*

These mean that in order to solve a problem you must first understand the relationships amongst the problem's key components.

Sun Tzu says: *Rouse him, and learn the principle of his activity or inactivity. Force him to reveal himself, so as to find out his vulnerable spots.*

This means probe the nature of the problem facing you. Study its history and setting; what makes this problem different or similar to other problems or experiences you have previously encountered?

Sun Tzu says: *When a warlike prince attacks a powerful state, his generalship shows itself in preventing the concentration of the enemy's forces. He overawes his opponents, and their allies are prevented from joining against him.*

This means that separating and isolating manageable parts of the problem is a key to keeping the problem solvable. Solve critical parts of the problem first, and the balance will fall in your direction.

Sun Tzu says: *We are not fit to lead an army on the march unless we are familiar with the face of the country—its mountains and forests, its pitfalls and precipices, its marshes and swamps. We shall be unable to turn natural advantage to account unless we make use of the local guides.*

This means that without knowledge of the issues, and without understanding of the problem you face, you cannot allocate your resources effectively. The answers are waiting for you; ask questions and the answers will become your guides.

Sun Tzu says: *The rules of the military are five: measurement, assessment, calculation, balancing, and victory. Measurement owes its existence to Earth; estimation of quantities to measurement; calculation to estimation of quantity; balancing of chances to calculation; and victory to balancing of chances.*

This means that studying and assessing a problem are the primary tools of problem solving. All points on the path of a successful solution start with an accurate assessment of the problem itself. Objective analysis is key to the early stages of understanding, but victory requires synthesis.

Sun Tzu says: *The control of a large force is the same principle as the control of a few men: it is merely a question of dividing up their numbers.*

This means that if faced with a complex problem, break it down into small, more manageable issues. Large and small issues are only a matter of dimension or scale.

Sun Tzu says: *Hence a wise general makes a point of foraging on the enemy.*

This means that many aspects of the solution you seek lie within the problem itself. Come to the problem unburdened by preconceptions and use the information you gather along the way to guide you.

It seems that we are reaching a point of congruence between our strategies and those of Sun Tzu for finding and solving problems. It also seems that Sun Tzu spent a huge portion of his preciously sparse book on the importance of understanding the system. We have agreed with him that this ability is the most tangible indication that a warrior will actually succeed.

Mr. Sun jots down an email to the Packer coaches to remind them that maybe a deep drop from the middle linebacker would help to solve their problem. We leave him to his work to begin our study of how we can effectively find problems worthy of our attention.

Step 4: Finding Problems

So my belief structure is like a three-legged stool. What if I end up with six or seven stools? What do I sit on?
Megan Kramer, Falconer Class of 2001

If there was a place along our path where my own students, year after year, wanted to stop, take a timeout, and really argue, it is right here. Our training and intuition both scream at us: "Why do I need to go looking for problems? Enough problems find me on their own!" Our educational system is firmly grounded in the concept that problem *solving* is the key to winning the game of life and that our daily encounters with the world provide us plenty of problems to solve, thanks very much.

So I will tell you what I used to tell my students at this point: *the central failure* of our entire educational system is that we provide canned material for students to solve and expect them to return to us the correct canned answer. That is *not* how the real world works; that is *not* how real problems occur that need to be solved. If we, as parents, teachers, and bosses, want our children, students, and employees to become more than robotic transponders of our historical and cultural ethos, we must teach them how to find their own problems in their own ways. Take a few more steps around this bend, and it will make sense.

*　　　*　　　*　　　*

The Lesson of Problems

Spring came early to the valley. By the middle of March, rolling green pastures carpeted the valley floor, and wildflowers grew in the warm sunlight. The distant mountains still held caps of white snow to remind us of long nights and winter's cold. Just outside the classroom window, the broad old oak tree shaded the small schoolyard; robins, perched on its thick limbs, called to one another. Spring is every child's favorite time of the school year, because everything seems a little happier, and because summer vacation is not very far away.

On that late spring morning, Mr. Usher sat behind his big wooden desk, his chin resting on his hand, frowning. He absently watched a couple of big flies buzz lazily against a closed window in the morning sunlight. The Children worked at their desks, occasionally giggling and passing notes and doing all of those things that we like to do when the teacher's not paying too much attention.

Max nudged Schuyler and pointed to Mr. Usher. Max was a good boy who almost never misbehaved or got in trouble or was scolded by Mr. Usher. Maybe this was because he didn't like to be scolded, but I think it was also because he kept an eye on Mr. Usher and knew when to be on his absolutely best behavior.

"Look at Mr. Usher frowning," whispered Max. "It's not like him to frown unless he's angry about something, but he doesn't look angry. What do you think is wrong?"

"I don't know," Schuyler whispered back, hunching his shoulders over and going back to work. Schuyler was often warned by Mr. Usher to pay attention and not bother the other Children, and he didn't want to draw Mr. Usher's attention to himself that morning.

"It just doesn't seem right," said Max. "I think I'll ask him."

Since it was a sunny spring day and the class was quiet and well behaved, and since Max was at heart a curious boy, that's exactly what he did.

Max stood up from his desk and ruffled his papers quietly. Mr. Usher frowned all the harder at the buzzing flies. Max cleared his throat and raised his hand part way. "Excuse me, Mr. Usher," he said quietly. "I have a question."

Mr. Usher looked up at Max slowly as if he'd been taking a nap and was just waking up. "Yes Max, what is it?" Mr. Usher asked. The frown had disappeared from his face.

"Well, it's nothing really. I was just wondering why you're frowning that way. It's a beautiful day and no one in class is misbehaving, but you don't look very happy."

Mr. Usher looked at Max, and then around at the other Children, who by now had all placed their pencils on their desks and were looking intently back at Mr. Usher. Mr. Usher grinned and adjusted his glasses, which frequently slipped down on his nose when he had been thinking too hard, or when he had his head down to read from a book. The Children, and especially Max, relaxed at seeing Mr. Usher smile.

"Max, you're absolutely right, but you've got it turned upside down. You see, I *don't* have a problem and that's precisely why I'm unhappy. I'm always a lot happier when I have lots of problems."

Max stood silently by his desk and fidgeted with his hands and frowned down at his books as if they might give him a better answer. All of the

Children looked at Mr. Usher, and most of them frowned as well, or chewed on their lips or wrinkled their brows. Max looked back up at Mr. Usher and said quite directly, "I don't get it."

Mr. Usher leaned back in his chair, then pressed his hands down on his desk and stood up tall against the blackboard. He walked around the front of his desk and sat down on the corner, crossing his long arms over his chest. "No, I don't suppose you do," said Mr. Usher. "But it's really not too difficult to understand if I just explain it properly. Let's all gather 'round and get comfortable and talk about it."

So that's what they did. The Children knew Mr. Usher quite well, and whenever he told them to gather 'round and get comfortable, they know they were in for some kind of a special treat, though Mr. Usher's treats were often of the kind that took some time to understand. When all the Children had pulled their desks in closely around Mr. Usher, with a great deal of scuffling and shuffling (and a bit of pushing since we all like to be at the front when a treat is coming) and the Children had all quieted down so you could hear the big bottle flies bumping and buzzing against the window panes, Mr. Usher began.

"Max asked why I wasn't happy, and I said it was because I don't have any problems. And that's true. I'm never as happy as when I have lots of problems, at least the right kind of problems anyway. Problems, you see, can be some of your best friends."

Schuyler raised his hand and Mr. Usher nodded at him. "*I'm* not happy when I have problems. If I'm late for school or don't clean my room or don't do my homework, I get in trouble. That's a problem and it's not fun at all," said Schuyler. All of the Children nodded their heads and noisily agreed that problems were *not* any fun.

Mr. Usher smiled and winked at some of the Children. "First let's decide what we're talking about." With that, Mr. Usher turned back to the chalkboard and drew a big line straight down the middle.

"Let's make a list of all the problems you can think of, or at least enough to fill up the left side of the blackboard. It shouldn't be hard. We all have problems every day."

Slowly at first and then seemingly all at once, the Children raised their hands, and Mr. Usher wrote down their problems. How quickly the list grew!

mean big brothers
broccoli
too late for the school bus
worn out shoes
bullies in the schoolyard
rainy days with nothing to do

no money for the movies on Saturday afternoon
early bedtimes
long division

And on and on until finally Mr. Usher was down on one knee, writing in tiny letters, and the left hand side of the blackboard was filled with all of the problems the Children could think of.

Mr. Usher straightened up with his hand pressed against his back, wincing a bit, because he's not very young anymore and his back almost always seems to be hurting him. "Let's work on the right side of the chalkboard now," Mr. Usher said, moving to the top again with his chalk poised to write. "I'll go first. I've just thought of a problem that I didn't think of a few minutes ago, even though it was right in front of my face. My problem is that I don't understand why bottle flies keep bumping into that closed window instead of flying out of the open window across the room. Those flies will bump against that closed window until they drop dead at the bottom, when all they have to do is fly around the room a bit, and surely they'd find their way out somewhere."

So Mr. Usher wrote on the top of the right side of the blackboard:

Why do flies keep bumping closed windows?

Now all of us have watched flies do just that and have perhaps wondered the very same thing ourselves. But the Children only looked at each other, puzzled. Finally, Aneal raised her hand.

"That's not the same thing as the other problems," she said. "The other problems are *real* problems. They make you sad, or you get hurt, or punished, or in trouble. *Your* problem is just a question that you're curious about."

Mr. Usher grinned more broadly. "Exactly. Now help me finish my side of the black board. I really do need help because I seem to have run out of my kind of problems, at least for the moment."

The Children looked blankly at Mr. Usher, and then at each other, and then back at Mr. Usher. Finally Aneal raised her hand again, slowly, as if she were not at all sure of herself. Mr. Usher called on her.

"This is probably going to sound really silly, but I've always wondered why airplanes fly. I'm sure there's a good reason, but I don't know what it could be. They look as if they'll fall out of the sky at any moment because they don't flap their wings like a bird or a bee or a butterfly."

Mr. Usher wrote

Why do airplanes fly?

Casey stood up suddenly from his desk. "This is easy." Casey often talked without being called on, which usually annoyed Mr. Usher, but in this case Mr. Usher didn't seem to mind. Casey had an excited look in his eyes. "You're just writing questions. All right, what's 14,872,329 times eleven?" The Children giggled and elbowed each other because everyone knew that Casey was crazy about math problems, and most of them didn't think Mr. Usher would add a math problem to the list on the blackboard.

Mr. Usher calmly wrote

What is 14,872,329 × 11?

and turned back to the class. The Children who had been giggling at Casey a moment before weren't laughing any longer.

"Next?" Mr. Usher asked.

Morgan, who had been sitting at the back of the class, hadn't giggled at Casey's math problem. She stood up, hand half raised, looking back and forth at the long list on the left side of the board and the short list on the right side of the board. Mr. Usher called on her.

"I don't know if this is right, but it seems like some of the problems we listed on the left side of the board need to be on the right side as well. I mean look at number three over there," she said, pointing at the long left-hand list.

3. bullies

"We said bullies were a problem because bullies start fights and hurt people for no reason. We could put the same problem on the right side of the board. I've always wondered why some kids fight. I mean, it always ends up badly and everyone either gets hurt or gets in trouble or is sad, so why do they do it? Or look at number 1."

1. broccoli for dinner

"My parents tell me we have to eat all of our vegetables or we won't grow up big and strong. But we almost never eat *all* of our vegetables, and we're still pretty big and pretty strong. My big brother is on the football team and he's *really* strong, and he doesn't eat all of *his* vegetables."

Mr. Usher was writing furiously on the right side of the blackboard to keep up with Morgan. He wrote

Why do kids fight?
and
What if we didn't eat any vegetables?

and

How many vegetables do we have to eat to be big and strong?

And when he turned back around to face the Children, almost all of their hands were in the air. Mr. Usher wrote as fast as he could while the Children called out their problems:

Why don't ducks have teeth?
What makes lightning?
How come glue sticks?
Do dogs talk when they bark?
Why is a blackboard green?
Why do people from different countries speak different languages?

Soon Mr. Usher was down on one knee again writing in tiny letters at the bottom of the chalkboard, and the right side of the board was as full as the left.

Again Mr. Usher stood up, wincing as he stretched his back, and patting the chalk dust off of his fingers. He sat back down on the front of his desk, gave a heavy sigh, and smiled. "Here's the treat, Children. Listen carefully and think about what you've just taught yourselves. At first when I asked you about problems, you thought only about things that make you mad or sad or get you in trouble. Then you saw that there are other kinds of problems that don't have bad endings, which just mean you're curious or interested. In fact, just by looking at some of those 'bad' problems a little bit differently, you turned them into 'good' problems! Those good problems are now nothing more than questions that we want answers to! And we all know that once we have answers, a lot of problems just disappear.

"This morning I was puzzled because, as a teacher, I want to always learn more and more. In order to learn I have to answer questions. In order to answer questions, I have to have questions to answer. And in order to have questions, it really helps to have …"

Mr. Usher paused, looked at the Children, and all in one voice they shouted,

"Problems!"

"So," Mr. Usher asked, smiling to himself at how quickly the Children had understood his lesson, "should we be afraid of problems? Do problems *always* make us sad or mad, or get us in trouble?" The Children all shook their heads or answered "no," and some of them had a little smile as if they had just received a little extra allowance for no reason at all.

"No, indeed," continued Mr. Usher. "Problems are what make us interested to learn more. Problems are the sign of a curious or creative mind. Problems are really just challenges and opportunities in disguise. People who go looking for interesting problems are people who create and invent and discover things. Someone who never looks for problems will rarely learn anything new. And the 'bad' problems, the kind that truly do make you mad or sad or get you into trouble, well, try to turn them into 'good' problems by asking questions about them, or looking at them from a different direction. You'll see how quickly some of those 'bad' problems will disappear."

With that, Mr. Usher asked the Children to push their desks back into line, which took a while because at least some of the Children were thinking hard about what they had learned. But soon the classroom was back in order and the lunch bell rang, and everyone rushed out of doors to enjoy the warm, sunny spring day. The robins in the oak tree had been joined by several noisy blue jays that screeched rudely to the Children as they spread their lunches around on the dry grass in the big oak's shade. Perhaps it was just a coincidence, but during that lunch hour, no one got into a fight or argued over a spot in the shade, and no one was late getting back into class.

*   *   *   *

Congratulations! Our reader has been wonderfully patient and persistent to arrive at this juncture. We are now at the very center of strategic and creative thinking: *Problem Finding*. Most of our education and training emphasizes solving problems, or finding the answers to existing questions and then doing something with that answer. This "solution management" is what follows from this point forward, at least until that unfortunate point where we encounter a train wreck, but let's leave that for the last chapter. One must ask the question, then: What *precedes* problem solving? Surely if problem solving is so important, then the step immediately prior must be critical.

It is obvious that before solving a problem, we must have a problem to solve, and as Mr. Usher taught us, we should constantly be on the lookout for new problems to solve: thus Problem Finding. Since we are perched exactly on the fulcrum of the teeter-totter of this book, we might as well look backward as well as forward just to make sure our reader knows there is some method to the model.

What precedes finding a problem? We know that we cannot coherently describe a problem if we do not understand that which we are observing, what we've called a system. And we cannot honestly pretend to know that which we are observing if we do not acknowledge the relationship between the observer and the observed, thus the discussion of subjectivity and objectivity. We cannot understand this relationship unless we have the ability to ask questions and understand the pitfalls that await us if we question without a plan. And surely we are not in a position to confront the world around us if we are not prepared in mind and soul to do so. Finally, seeing how potentially challenging this whole process might be, we would hardly wish to accept it if we had not found a very tangible reason to do so. Most of us find this compelling reason embodied in a hero whom we want to emulate or an image of our future self that we want to be. It is the conscious and unconscious lessons we have learned from these heroes that give us the desire and energy to undertake such a process.

That, in a nutshell, is the nexus at which we have arrived. Without problems we have no questions and no answers. By definition, therefore, problems are good things to be sought out and managed. Without problems, the world is a static place indeed. We cannot rise to a next level. We can't create, inspire, innovate, invent, pioneer, expand, grow, or transcend. In other words, we can't do any of the things that our heroes did to make them our heroes.

So what creates a problem? Why is something problematic? Where do problems come from?

Dissonance

Problems are caused by *dissonance*. Dissonance can be defined as a lack of harmony or agreement. A musical chord is dissonant if one of the notes is not in harmony with the others. It sounds wrong to our ears. We want or expect to hear something sweet and harmonious; if we hear a note out of harmony, we hear dissonance. We have a problem with the way the chord sounds, not because the sound is inherently bad or wrong, but because it does not sound the way we wanted or expected it to sound.

This then is the root of problems: the difference between the way something *is* and the way we *want or expect it to be*.

Real learning, whether in the classroom or the real world, occurs when an individual takes a personal stake in solving a problem that is meaningful to him or her. The person finds a visceral, tangible difference between the world as they expect or want it to be and the world as it is. They will wrestle and prod and provoke the problem, using all of their tools and resources, until they either resolve the conflict to a point of satisfaction or just give up. Dissonance immediately leads to questioning: we ask "why," "why not," and "what if" until answers of satisfactory magnitude are found that either eliminate the dissonance or decrease it to a level of acceptability.

Dissonance leads to evolution and to revolution. It can be benign or destructive.

Scientists build questions on top of preceding results because the result does not fully eradicate the dissonance: something still does not fit. Our understanding of the world evolves through this process. Individuals and societies revolt when they viscerally believe that the world does not meet their expectations, when the contrast between their own circumstances and those of rulers or colonial powers are so marked as to create a flammable dissonance.

Good teachers ensure that their students learn the subject material to an acceptable or superior level. Great teachers all do one thing well: *they create dissonance in the minds of their students and guide them in the resolution of that dissonance.* This is not always an easy path, particularly for young people. There may be anxiety, timidity, or tears when the student finds out that the world is not as simple or sugarcoated as Mommy and Daddy, Grandma and the babysitter, big sister and the storyteller had led him to believe. But the process results in real learning, a growing ability to face and overcome complex obstacles for which there may be no canned answer or pretty roadmap.

In all cases dissonance, the recognition that "I" have a problem, leads first to questioning and then to growth of knowledge or experience. The individual is directly, in some cases, passionately involved, self-interested in the outcome, in finding answers and more questions and more answers until the dissonance is reduced to an acceptable level. This is the true process of learning. It can be tumultuous, exciting, uplifting, rocky, enlightening, or all of them at once.

The first half of the teeter-totter is now behind us, and we have crossed the fulcrum. We know who we want to be, how to prepare, how we view the world, how to wrestle problems from our surroundings, and how to analyze that which we observe. Time to get some answers.

Step 5: Solving Problems

You can build your life on a foundation that you can easily crumble whenever you choose.
Laura Katz, Falconer Class of 2000

As I have suggested throughout the first half of this book, problem solving is the foundational element of most of modern Western education. The Progressive Education movement of the late nineteenth and early twentieth centuries was based on the concept of teaching young people to think and manipulate information, instead of just regurgitating solutions. It was a revolutionary step forward, and we continue to place the highest level of importance on the ability to solve the important and meaningful problems that life throws at us. What we have tried to demonstrate on our path so far is the critical nature of all that goes before the process of effectively arriving at a satisfactory solution. Problem solving is a very necessary *reaction* that follows the *proactive* steps that we have already taken. And now that we are ready, we can tackle something meaningful when it comes our way.

*   *   *   *

The Lesson of the Mountain

The Children loved summer school. All during the regular school year, they sat through long hours in the classroom, waiting for lunchtime and recess, and even though Mr. Usher tried his best to keep class lively and interesting, even he couldn't keep school from being bothersome sometimes. But in the summer, the Children came to school for only part of the day, and as often as not Mr. Usher would hold class out of doors in the shade of the old oak tree, and sometimes the Children and he would just talk or read on the cool, dry grass. Sometimes one or more of the Children would lie back and close his or her eyes for a few minutes, and Mr. Usher would pretend not to notice. Summer school didn't even seem like school to the Children, yet at the end of each summer some of them thought that they might have learned more during summer than during the whole rest of the year.

The real treat of summer school came each June or July when Mr. Usher announced The Outing. The Children loved (as I'm sure you all do as well) to travel around the countryside in summer to get away from home for a few days and to see new places. Each summer Mr. Usher would take the Children somewhere special by train or by bus for two or three days, or even for as long as a week. They'd visited museums and theaters and parks and monuments and farms on past Outings, and each had been more exciting than the last. Each summer the Children couldn't wait for Mr. Usher to tell them about The Outing, so they could think and plan and look forward to it, almost like getting ready for Christmas or for one's birthday party.

So it was that one breezy day in late June, as the Children sat and sprawled on the grass under the old oak tree, I heard Mr. Usher ask them to all gather 'round as he had something important to discuss.

The Children moved into a semicircle, and Mr. Usher wheeled a tack board out from the classroom and set it in front of the Children. On the tack board was a large map, and since most of the Children had paid attention in their geography lessons, they quickly recognized the curving rivers, broad hills, and deep valleys of Mountain Park.

"We've had many interesting Outings over the years," Mr. Usher began, "but I think you're going to *especially* enjoy *this* Outing. We're going to Mountain Park for a three-day camping trip. We'll carry our tents and our food and our sleeping bags and see as much of the park as we can. What do you think?"

For a moment the Children sat, staring at the map, not really believing what he had told them, and then all at once they cheered and shouted and clapped their hands and told Mr. Usher that it was a perfect idea and they couldn't wait to go. Some of the Children had been to Mountain Park before, and these told the other Children excitedly how it was the most beautiful place they'd ever seen, how tall the mountains were, and how cold the rivers, until finally Mr. Usher held up his hand again for quiet.

"We'll go next week. We have a lot of work to do to prepare."

For the rest of that day and the two days following, Mr. Usher and the Children discussed all of the things they needed to prepare for such an exciting Outing. They studied the map and decided which trails to take. They wrote lists of things that each person should bring and more lists of things that might be shared, and decided what to buy and what to borrow. They talked about the trees and plants and animals they might see, about which were friendly or helpful and which should be left alone. Finally, the day before The Outing was to begin, the Children were as prepared as they would ever be, and they all went home to get a good night's rest and dream about the fun days ahead.

We needn't go into all of the details of how they met together the first day and packed their things onto the bus and noisily argued about who should sit where for the trip to Mountain Park, or of how they drove across the green farm lands of the great open valley. It's enough to say that after a long day of traveling, just as the sun slipped below the tall mountain peaks on the western side of the valley with all of the hillsides bathed in a golden early-evening glow, they arrived at the entrance to Mountain Park. The Children gratefully tumbled out of the cramped bus and ran amongst the tall pine trees, smelling the fresh mountain air and tossing about great handfuls of dry brown pine needles until finally Mr. Usher called them back and had them make camp for the night.

In small groups of threes and fours, the Children set out the tents, rolled out sleeping bags, collected wood, and started fires for cooking. They drew water from Clear Creek, which babbled noisily past the campground, and prepared dinner and did all of the many things that one must do when one is having a camping adventure. Unlike at home, where these jobs would all be chores and we would grumble and moan about doing them, here on a great Outing in the mountains it seemed like a big game, and all of the Children pitched in and helped. Sooner than you would think, they'd all eaten a wonderful supper, the tents and sleeping bags were set out, and all of the Children and Mr. Usher sat around a roaring big campfire watching sparks float up towards the millions of stars spread out across the clear mountain sky. Mr. Usher told them stories from long ago of how the mountains were made and how the animals came to live in the forest, and even though they were just stories and not really true, the Children enjoyed them.

"Tomorrow," said Mr. Usher, "we'll follow the trail beside Clear Creek. The next day we'll go over the mountains and then follow Rocky Brook back down to the Raging River. The bus will be parked there waiting for us. But that's a long way to walk, so everyone off to bed now and sleep well because tomorrow will be a long, long day."

The Children all found their own tents and crawled into their warm sleeping bags, and one by one their flashlights winked out around the campground. For a few more minutes, the Children talked and whispered to their tent mates and wiggled around to get more comfortable (since most of them were not used to sleeping in tents on the ground), but soon even the whispers died away. Mr. Usher banked the fire with dirt and spread out the burning branches until only the dark red embers glowed, and by then the only thing one could hear in all of the great forest was Clear Creek tumbling its way past the sleeping children and an occasional bullfrog croaking to its neighbors.

In the morning, the early chatter of noisy blue jays awakened the Children. Earlier than any of us would have been out of bed at home, they had eaten breakfast, packed their sturdy backpacks, and eagerly awaited Mr. Usher's direction to start out on the trail. They set off at a steady pace, in single file and in pairs, along the well-worn path, with Clear Creek on their right-hand side and the mountains, glimpsed here and there between the pine trees as they walked, on their left-hand side. Occasionally someone would stop to rest, or take a drink from the creek, or pause to look at some particularly pretty flower or interesting plant. Squirrels scampered across the trail and up tall pine trees, flicking their thick, bushy tails and chattering at the Children as they passed by underneath.

After hiking for what seemed like many miles, and with the sun shining down fiercely from high overhead, Mr. Usher called to the Children to look for a nice place to stop for lunch. Soon they found a great spread of broad, flat rocks touching the creek. The Children thankfully set down their heavy packs, slipped off their shoes and socks, and hungrily ate their midday meal. Some hung their feet off of the rocks into the chilly water, and others lay back on the warm rocks in the sun while they talked about what they had seen during the morning. Before any of the Children were completely ready, Mr. Usher roused them and told them that they still had quite a way to go, and off they started once again along the trail.

All afternoon they hiked, with Clear Creek always on their right and the mountains always on their left, gradually climbing higher and closer to the mountains. The forest became less dense and the trees shorter as they climbed in the thinning air. The creek grew narrower and steeper and tumbled over large rocks in long white strings of rapids. On the Children hiked, their legs growing weary and their shoulders aching from the weight of the packs. By late in the afternoon, as they climbed very near to the base of the highest peaks, Clear Creek shrank to a small stream that one could easily cross on the rocks without getting one's feet wet. Chilly shadows from the low afternoon sun crept up the sides of the mountains.

Suddenly, the trail stopped. Where a few minutes earlier the trail had been wide and well worn, here it merely disappeared at the end of a small, open, grassy meadow. A broken wall of rocks, and behind it the mountains rose steeply up, spread off both to the right and the left as far as the Children could see. The Children at the head of the group stopped and waited for Mr. Usher and the others to catch up. As Mr. Usher walked around the last bend in the trail before the meadow, Andy was the first to shout out.

"Mr. Usher," he called cupping his hands around his mouth, "the trail has stopped. There's nowhere to go. What do we do now?"

Mr. Usher walked up to the end of the trail, and the Children gathered around him. He looked ahead at the rocks and the mountain.

"Well, you're certainly right," Mr. Usher said. "The trail has stopped. What do *you* suggest we do?"

"*We* don't know what to do," Andy answered. "You're the teacher. Tell us where to go."

"We've never been here before," added Felisa. "How are *we* supposed to know which way to go?"

"I'm ready for your suggestions," said Mr. Usher. "I'm not at all sure that there *is* any one best way to proceed here. Who has a good idea about what to do?"

Aaron, who had never been on holidays in the wilderness before, looked worried and said "We'll have to go back. We can't leave the trail." Andy, who fancied himself an experienced outdoorsman and had been leading the hikers much of the day, said, "That mountain doesn't look so high. Let's get going and we might be over it before dark." Michael, one of the quiet children who had been looking thoughtfully at the mountain, said, "It's getting late, and we don't really know what to do. Maybe the best thing would be to stop in this nice meadow for the night and talk things out, and tomorrow we'll have a full day to do whatever it is that we decide."

The Children were all very tired and hungry from their long hike, and the cozy green meadow with its soft grass and the small upper reaches of Clear Creek streaming cheerily through made a very inviting spot in which to spend the night. So that's what they did. Soon they had all eaten supper, the tents and sleeping bags were set out in rows on the banks of the creek, and the Children and Mr. Usher were sitting around a big crackling campfire, some close to the fire where it was toasty warm, and others farther back on the edges of the dancing ring of light. Mr. Usher cleared his throat for their attention.

"It seems we've run out of trail," he began, "or maybe the trail has run out on us. Either way, we have to decide what to do tomorrow."

Aaron (who you will remember had never been camping before) hugged his knees and looked up at Mr. Usher, worried. "If you knew the trail would end, why did you bring us this way?" he asked.

"I didn't know the trail would end here. In fact, I've never been up the trail this far. If I *had* been along the trail before, this would be a pretend adventure, not a real adventure, and you're all old enough for a real adventure on your summer Outing. In real life we don't always know what's going to happen next. We're already doing exactly what one should do when one first faces a new problem. We're sitting down calmly and thinking things out clearly. We should never rush at a problem or shoot off in the first direction that presents itself. Usually, doing nothing for a little while is a pretty good first step."

The Children look puzzled and a little doubtful, as if they weren't sure how doing nothing could help them whatsoever.

"So now that we're thinking clearly," continued Mr. Usher, "we need to decide if we really have a problem, and if so, what is it?"

Aaron hugged himself a little closer. "Well *I* think we have a problem. The map shows that we only have to cross the mountain to get to where we are going, but the mountain looks very steep and there's no trail to follow. If we go forward we may get lost. If we go back, it will take a whole day plus another day to walk to where the bus is supposed to meet us. But we have only one day's food left, and we'll be awfully hungry by the time we get there. That's the problem as I see it."

The Children murmured back and forth among themselves, and soon they all agreed that they certainly had a problem and that Aaron had expressed it very well.

Mr. Usher smiled at them. "You don't need any help at all," he said, playfully poking the nearest child in the ribs. "You've already taken the next step in solving a problem. You've all agreed what the problem *is*! That's usually the hardest part of all, (especially for grownups), and you came to an agreement in practically no time at all. The rest will be very easy to solve. I'm sure of it."

The Children brightened with Mr. Usher's confidence and praise, and some even smiled a little. Andy stood up and addressed the group. "I for one think we can get over that mountain. I don't want to go back without at least giving it a try, just because there's no clear trail. I say we try to get over the mountain tomorrow. If we fail, we can always go back the next day. Going hungry for two days shouldn't be that much worse than going hungry for one day. I say we go forward."

For a long time the Children talked back and forth about turning back or going ahead, and in the end they decided to give the mountain a try. "Well, then," said Mr. Usher, "I suggest we all get some sleep. Remember, when you're looking for an answer, all paths may look equally good, but they rarely are. Think and sleep on it, and tomorrow we'll try to find a way over the mountain."

So the Children went off to their own sleeping bags and tents, but this time they were so tired that it seemed that before they had even turned out their flashlights most had fallen fast asleep, and maybe some of them dreamed about tall mountains and fast-running streams, and whether their decision would seem less glorious on very empty stomachs.

The next morning after breakfast, the Children and Mr. Usher gathered at the end of the trail, gazing up at the solid gray mountain in front of them. It looked awfully tall and steep with many high cliffs and long slopes of broken rock. They could even see bits of old snow hiding in shady crevices high up on the slopes with small rivulets of water melting from the downhill edges.

"There's certainly no obvious trail, at least not one we can see from here," Mr. Usher said. "Often it helps to look at a problem from different angles. Let's spread out as widely as we can across the meadow and all take another look."

So the Children went off in groups of threes and fours all across the meadow, their necks craned back, searching hopefully for some sign of a way up the mountain. Soon they were joined together again in a group, talking all at once and pointing excitedly up the mountain.

"There's a flat ledge just over that ridge, way off to the left," Erin pointed. "It looks like it goes all the way up the mountain and right over to the other side."

"Over to the right is a long rock fall that doesn't look *too* awfully steep from where we were," said Kara. "Right near the top of the rock fall I think I saw a small path, maybe a deer trail that may go all the way across the mountain."

"I backed up across the meadow so I could see the forest in the center of the mountain more clearly," said Andy. "Once you go up the first part of these rocks right in front of us, I'm sure there's a path up through the trees."

The Children looked this way and that at each of the different possible ways up the mountain, pointing out the good spots and the bad spots of each. Most wanted to follow Andy's path in the middle because it looked like the closest and the easiest of all. Some of the Children started hoisting their packs onto their shoulders, ready to charge up and over the rocks in front of them.

Mr. Usher held up his hand and asked for quiet. "We should all remember that things aren't always exactly what they seem," he said. "If we all load up our packs and set off up the center path, and it proves to be the *wrong* path, then we'll have put all of our eggs into a single basket, and may end up wasting the entire day. Let's send out a small group to quickly scout each route. No heavy packs so you can walk more easily, and four in each group. If the trail doesn't go all the way to the next valley, your whole group should return. If it does go all the way, then two stay at the highest point of the trail, and the other two come back to report to the rest of us."

So the Children formed groups and some stayed behind with Mr. Usher, and off the groups ran, happy to be free of the heavy packs on their shoulders. Mr. Usher and the remaining children sat down by the cool water of Clear Creek to wait. They didn't have to wait for long. With a great noise and commotion, Andy's group came running and shouting back over the rocks.

"Bears!" Andy blurted out, gulping for breath. "A mother and two cubs, eating berries up in the trees, right in the middle of the trail. It's a good trail, and I could see that it goes all the way to the top of the mountain, but we can't get by those bears!"

Half an hour later, from the far left side of the meadow, Erin's group walked towards them, their heads down. "We followed the flat ledge up and over the ridge," Erin said. "It's a beautiful trail, and you can see clear back down the valley for miles and miles. But just as we came close to the top of the mountain, the ledge ended in a sheer cliff. There's no way up and no way around. We came so close, but it's just no good."

The Children hung their heads and looked down at their feet and wondered if they would *ever* find a good way over the mountain. "Come on now," chided Mr. Usher. "Don't look so glum. Don't give up hope. If you ever stop believing that you can solve a problem, then you'll surely fail."

Finally the last scout group walked into sight from the far side of the meadow. "We made it all the way to the top of the long rock slope, and there's a small path leading up the mountain," Kara said, with a long look on her face. "But it started going down again and into the forest. After we saw that it led crossways over to the trees and not up and over the mountain, we turned around and came back again. It's hopeless."

By this time the sun was creeping high into the sky, and the Children all knew that they would have to start the long hike back the way they had come, and with only half as much food as they needed for the trip. They all sat down and let out a big sigh.

"Now Children," Mr. Usher said a bit sternly, "I haven't brought you all this way so you can stop here and feel sorry for yourselves. Scouting paths and testing ideas would be a huge waste of time if we didn't learn anything from what we find when we scout and test. I want each of you to tell the others once again what you saw on your scouting trip this morning, and we'll all think hard and see if we've learned anything of use."

So Andy told again about the bears, Erin told again about the cliff, and Kara told again about the path that led side-hill into the trees. The Children put their hands in their chins and thought as hard as they could. Suddenly Schuyler jumped up and shouted out.

"I've got it! Andy's group came back first, so the bears must be low down on the mountain. Kara's trail goes into the forest, but much higher up the mountain. We can go up Kara's trail, follow it over to the forest path, and go right around those bears!"

"Excellent, Schuyler," Mr. Usher said, smiling and patting him on the back. "You used your head to solve a puzzle, and maybe we'll all be less hungry tonight because of it. But let's make sure we understand what we've decided, and how we'll make certain it comes out right in the end. We have to get around the bears, which means being very quiet and alert all the way to the top of the mountain. And we have to move quickly so the bears don't have a chance to move into our way on their own. Are we all agreed to move quickly and quietly and hike as strongly as we can together?"

The Children nodded. "All right, then," Mr. Usher said. "Remember, this is a real adventure, and we don't know for sure what lies up ahead. But once you've scouted every route, and used all the new information at hand, and made the best decision possible, then is the time to do your best to make sure your solution works."

So Mr. Usher and the Children loaded up their packs, started off across the meadow, and climbed up the mountain with Kara in the lead. The long slope of broken rock was slippery and steep, but even with their heavy packs and the hot sun overhead, the Children moved steadily upward. They walked as quietly as possible, though the sound of pebbles and stones skittering down the talus slope followed them ever upward. Finally the children reached the top of the rocky slope and moved on to the small deer path slanting towards the trees. They walked on as quietly as possible, though after the steep climb they would have loved to stop and talk and point at the beautiful scenery laid out far below them in the deep green valley.

Soon they were in amongst the pine trees that covered the center of the mountain. The forest was cool and shady and smelled of rich moist earth. They nervously kept watching for the bears. Suddenly, Kara froze in her tracks and pointed down through the trees. All of the hikers stopped as well and peered through the shadows and low-hanging branches to where Kara pointed. A short way down the slope, sitting in a patch of sun, a large brown bear and two cubs sat in the tall grass, peering lazily about and sniffing the air. As the Children stopped, the large bear seemed to stiffen and put her nose higher into the air as if she smelled something unusual in the forest. Creeping as quietly as small forest mice, the Children inched forward, one eye on the trail and one on the bears, in case the bears should suddenly charge. But the bears just sat in the sun, sniffed at the breeze, and rolled in the grass. If they ever heard the Children or smelled them, we don't know, because after a few minutes the bears were out of sight and the Children all let out a huge sigh of relief.

Soon the deer path ran across another trail that angled straight up the mountain. The Children once again turned uphill, quickening their pace as they all sensed that the top was near. And it was! The trees disappeared and all the Children saw ahead of them was a low ridge and blue mountain sky. They broke into a run and soon all of them were standing on top of the mountain looking far down the other side. A swift stream rushed down the mountainside, and along it a wide trail curved down to the valley. In the valley the stream joined a river, and beyond that, the road home.

The Children were eager to rush down the trail as if they thought the trail and road home might suddenly disappear, but Mr. Usher made them wait. "Take a moment to think about what we've done," he said. "We faced a real problem last night and today, and there weren't any mothers and fathers to help you, but you found a way through it. Maybe next time you have a problem you think is very difficult, you'll remember this mountain, and how you found a way over it."

So the Children rested a minute to drink in the beautiful view and think about what they had learned. Then, like a horse turned back to the barn who will always go faster when he knows home is waiting, the Children nearly flew down the trail towards the road. All afternoon they walked, and occasionally one of the Children would stumble for a step as he or she took his or her eyes off of the trail to gaze back up at the big mountain that they had conquered.

Once again, as the sun fell behind the mountains, the Children knew their long walk was nearly over. Their legs were tired and rubbery, and their feet were blistered and sore. Their shirts stuck to their backs from the long hot day, and their stomachs grumbled since they hadn't had a full meal since the morning. But before they knew it, they saw the end of the trail, and next to the trail, the bus parked facing towards home. The Children ran down the last few yards of the trail and put their packs on the bus and clambered aboard, and this time there was no squabbling whatsoever about who should sit where and with whom. That may have been because the Children had all shared a great adventure and had solved a great problem together and didn't feel like squabbling, but it was because the Children were about as tired as you've ever seen a group of Children in your life, and almost before the bus pulled away from the trail, many of the Children were fast asleep, as the bus wound it's way back home through the long valley night.

$$* \qquad * \qquad * \qquad *$$

High above the stream-cut meadow that Mr. Usher and the Children have recently escaped, Mr. Sun sits, feet dangling eerily over the edge of a crystalline granite precipice. While the meadow, the stream, the rock wall, and the lazily lumbering bear family are a very long way off, we are not surprised that Mr. Sun has been able to watch the class on this journey. Our guides are free to watch and join the path with us if and when they choose. We sit down on the cliff next to Mr. Sun and ask him to comment on what has transpired.

"Easy problems are easy to solve. We solve them in the due course of every day and most require little strategy. So we must concern ourselves with how to overcome difficult problems, when life really throws us a wicked curve or a nasty slider. Even Tony Gwynn could only solve *that* problem a third of the time. The fact of tough problems is that they are tough to solve. It takes a lot of work. Most people don't like hard work; they would rather the problem just went away. But that is not the way of the warrior, or in your parlance, the falconer. Even those young kids down there, with a little guidance from their teacher, solved a tough problem. So let's lay out a game plan that is simple to follow, and works, even if it takes some effort."

Where is the dissonance?

First, resist the urge to react. Nine times out of ten, we are trying to solve the wrong problem. Reaction without analysis and understanding will almost always result in an inadequate solution. It may be easy, but it won't be right. Remember where problems come from; dissonance. Find the dissonance.

What happened to the Children at the rock wall? They experienced the dissonance of not being able to see a clear path when they expected such a path to lie before them. The problem was not the rock wall, but the fact that the wall blocked their easy path home. This is a huge difference. Problems are not independent creatures. They exist relative to our perceptions of how we want the world to be.

Sun Tzu says: *To begin by bluster, but afterwards to take fright at the enemy's numbers, shows a supreme lack of intelligence.*

This means that overly aggressive or impatient reaction to the presentation of a problem leads to the loss of ability to use skills and resources.

What is the problem?

Once we clearly define the underlying dissonance, we can articulate the problem. For the Children, the problem became "the rock wall is lying between us and where we want to be." Is the wall itself the problem? No. The wall is just a pile of un-climbable rocks. Flying to the conclusion that the wall is the problem would be a wasteful mistake. And not to squander an unsubtle image, it would put the Children on the wrong path towards a solution. The second error of most failed attempts at problem solving is an inaccurate vision or articulation of the problem itself. Make sure the problem is stated correctly and then proceed.

Ask questions!

The first sign of reactive problem solving is a preponderance of statements as opposed to questions. If the answer is simple, it would not be a real problem! You cannot know whether to react or think; you cannot understand the system; you cannot posit solutions until you have asked sufficient questions to define the realm of possible and probable answers. Beware the answer that comes before the question is asked.

Sun Tzu says: *If he (your opponent) is taking his ease, give him no rest.*

This means exhaust all possibilities through thorough questioning and pursuit of options.

Know yourself.

Assess your strengths and weaknesses, your resources, or those of your group, before attempting a solution. Would Mr. Usher and the Children have entertained different options if they had more or less food? More or fewer numbers? Someone hurt and unable to walk? A fast runner? Better or worse camping equipment? A radio? Fewer hours in the day? Better or worse knowledge of the mountain or the direction home?

A SWOT (Strength, Weakness, Opportunities, Threats) analysis takes time. When surprised in the open by a hungry lion, we do not have time to make this analysis. To the extent that we are prepared with self-knowledge before the attack, our chances of survival through reaction are greatly increased. When confronted with a problem that allows for thought, we must make time to carefully understand and calculate our resources.

Sun Tzu says: *When, in the consequence of heavy rains up-country, a river which you wish to ford is swollen and flecked with foam, you must wait until it subsides.*

This means that sometimes patience is your best resource. Do not try to accomplish everything at once. As conditions change, take time to reevaluate your options.

Know the enemy.

We now have tools to understand the problem, the same tools we used to understand a cubic meter of forestland or an island rain forest. We do our best, within the time and resource constraints of the problem, to understand the strengths and weaknesses of the problem, to know its nature. If we have time and resources on our side, we can make a more thorough assessment. If not, we will have to rely more heavily on our instincts. But what are instincts except the relict shadows of previous experience? Is not experience one of our greatest assets? If we have practiced this approach in the past, we will be prepared to make rapid assessments. If we have not practiced, we will be left to thoughtless reaction in an emergency.

Sun Tzu says: *If his forces are united, separate them.*
This means: separate and isolate large complex problems into small, manageable problems.

Sun Tzu says: Force him to reveal himself so as to find out his vulnerable spots.
This means understand the strengths and weaknesses of the problem.

Define the problem in terms of a goal.

This seems obvious, but it is the most common misstep of problem solving. If you don't know where you want to be, how can you get there? Knowing the true scope of your problem and your resources to solve it, determine one or more acceptable outcomes. For Mr. Usher and the Children, the goal was *not* to get over the mountain that lay in their path. The goal was to get home safely before their food ran out. These are *very* different goals. Before you posit solutions, you must have a clearly defined and correct goal.

Sun Tzu says: *If there is a disturbance in the camp, the general's authority is weak.*

This means that we need to clearly define goals and a vision before we start to solve problems. If the goals are not clear, resources will be wasted. Disorganization in the process of setting and communicating goals is reflective of a disorganized leader.

Brainstorm solutions.

Now we think of possible solutions. The more time we have, the more broadly we can think; we have the luxury of proposing solutions that may be wildly outside the box, high risk but high reward. The less time and more pressing the problem, the more we must constrain our thinking, focusing on the most probable successful outcomes.

In a true brainstorm, with no limit on their food and safety, the Children could have proposed telepathic communication with the mountain search and rescue squad, or reliance on manna from heaven to feed them. Both of these are possible but highly improbable solutions based on their true knowledge of the problem. If they had enough food to last a long while, they could have tested these improbable answers, and, lacking success, still been able to try something more practical. Given the reality of their situation, they did not have the luxury of testing a wide range of solutions. They focused on a small set of practical options, each with a reasonable probability of success.

On the other hand, one doubts that Charles Darwin would have solved the problem of the Galapagos finches without considering radical potential solutions. The natural selection of species was probably not the first thing that jumped into his mind with *HMS Beagle* lying at anchor, rocking in the gentle Pacific swell. But given time to explore a wide range of options, no matter how revolutionary, he came to an elegant solution and therefore takes his spot as one of our great problem-solving heroes.

Sun Tzu says: *Indirect tactics, efficiently applied, are inexhaustible as Heaven and Earth, unending as the flow of rivers and streams; like the sun and moon, they end but to begin anew; like the four seasons, they pass away to return once more.*

This means that the number of options that lie outside the realm of orthodox method are infinite compared to the number of options and pathways that lie inside this realm. Dead ends are not failures; they are another possible solution explored and rejected. Thinking creatively and without preconception opens up a nearly limitless number of possible solutions.

Understand possible outcomes.

Assess the strengths, weaknesses, and implied results of each possible solution. Do a check:

- Does it solve the defined problem?

- Does it achieve the goal?

- Do I have sufficient resources to achieve the result?

- Can I live with the successful outcome?

- What is the probability of success?

- Can I survive failure?

Then, make a choice.

Sun Tzu says: *The skillful tactician may be likened to a snake. Strike at its head, and you will be attacked by its tail; strike at its tail, and you will be attacked by its head; strike at its middle, and you will be attacked by head and tail both.*

This means that a good solution requires flexibility in response to both foreseen and unforeseen obstacles. Problems can be elegant in their complexity. Your solution should be more elegant than the problem you are solving.

Act.

Once we have made our assessment, if this takes a minute or a year, we must act with the confidence that we have done everything possible in order to ensure success. Now is not the time for timidity. While the possibility of failure is always real, it is far less if we act decisively, if we commit our armies fully to the battle. Does this mean that we never change our course? Once committed for a penny, are we destined to bet the mortgage? No. Difficult problems are rarely solved by a single action, and if we are in a corner where a single action may result in either complete victory or complete failure, perhaps we made a wrong decision somewhere in the past to get into this pickle in the first place.

We continue to watch and assess and make course corrections, as the Children did when they saw the bears lying athwart their path. But we also cannot let fear of the unknown, doubt, or uncertainty freeze us into inaction. Without action all of our work is just so much tacking into the teeth of a nasty gale.

Sun Tzu says: *Rapidity is the essence of war: take advantage of the enemy's unreadiness, make your way by unexpected routes, and attack unguarded spots.*

This means that once the solution is determined, act. Stay ahead of the problem, creating options to deal with the results in advance of the issues at hand.

Sun Tzu says: *Therefore, just as water retains no constant shape, so in warfare there are no constant conditions.*

This means that creativity, adaptation, and flexibility are the skills of problem solving, and they all require action.

A cool late afternoon breeze blows up-valley, ruffling the papers we have studied, and long shadows are cast over our shoulders by the peaks at our back. Mr. Sun squints into the distance and tells us that the Children are fast asleep on their bus as it winds its way down the mountain road. We cannot see nearly this far but have become accustomed to Mr. Sun's apparent ability to transcend our story's dimensions. We refer back to the list of directives about how to solve problems.

"We understand that solving hard problems takes work," we say. "But this seems a lot to ask. Will anyone really make this kind of effort? Take this time? Have this degree of patience? Aren't you asking quite a bit of the average person?"

Mr. Sun turns slowly towards us. His face is smiling, but his eyes are steely and much more purposeful than we are used to.

"Yes. That is precisely why there are many foot soldiers and falcons in the world, but few generals, falconers, or warriors. Let each choose what she or he wants to be."

Step 6: When Problems Don't Want to Be Solved

Conquest is sweet, like this pineapple.
Mark Shtayerman, Falconer Class of 1999

The respectful mind notes and welcomes differences between human individuals and between human groups, tries to understand these "others," and seeks to work effectively with them.
Howard Gardner, *Five Minds for the Future*

We find ourselves walking along a low, dimly lit tunnel with the smell of sweat, old leather, gun oil, and dirt seeping from the concrete walls. Yellow bulbs in wire cages light the way through shadows that obscure the way behind. We come to an iron door upon which a sign has been riveted:

SO MUCH FOR THE EASY STUFF

Despite our faith that these dioramas in which we find ourselves are all a fiction or a dream, we swallow nervously. No one enjoys dark fatalism on a welded iron door.

Opening the door, we find ourselves in something akin to a large square locker room, if only gymnasia had locker rooms assigned to the visiting team from hell. A narrow wooden bench is bolted into the four concrete walls. Above the bench every form of battle gear imaginable hangs on thick iron hooks, from prehistoric stone axes, curved scimitars, leather armor, and ash lances to polished machine pistols, fragmentation grenades, land mines, and lasers. The room looks like a museum garage sale gone horribly wrong or a costume wardrobe for a movie about time-traveling terrorists. We peer around a corner, where the showers or toilets ought to be. Three walls of this side room are stacked floor-to-ceiling with heavy wooden bookcases crammed with legal texts, dark leather-bound spines with gold leaf and scarlet ribbons bleeding from the shelves. On the fourth wall musty black judges' robes hang like darkroom drapes, a framed piece of parchment with the word "Constitution" printed in Old English across the top leans against the wall, and a box of handcuffs and sturdy oak gavels sits on the floor.

Mr. Sun stands in one corner, fastening a bronze breastplate across his thick leather fighting clothes, his long bow and razor-sharp sword already set aside and ready for their work. On the bench beside him is a very thin paperback book that, were it not for its modern-looking cover, we would have mistaken for his copy of the *Art of War*. We are utterly puzzled and turn to Mr. Sun for some direction.

"You have made it through the model to a point where we have to face reality," he says, cinching tight a leather helmet with the dark feathers of a peregrine sewn to the brow. "No matter how hard we prepare and try, no matter how well we play the game, there are times and places and systems that defy our efforts at solution. There are problems that don't want to be solved. It is imperative that we study two scenarios that may result from an unsatisfactory attempt at problem solving: conflict that can be avoided and conflict that cannot be avoided."

The massive display of armament in the locker room is pretty self-explanatory within this context; the adjoining room of law books and robes and the small paperback are not. We ask him about these.

"In ancient China we recognized the dangers of physical conflict; you will discuss later some of my comments in this regard. But we had not fully studied and understood the methodology of resolving conflict short of war. That's why the warlord consulting business was so good and the mediation business a bit thin back then. In more recent times, you have defined a system of rules by which a great deal of physical conflict can be avoided: you call it the law. Law protects innocent people from the free will of criminals, but even civil law is often a form of controlled confrontation that frequently does little to benefit either side, other than to make lawyers rich.

"You have started to solve this problem of physical and legal battling. You have widely read this excellent book by Messrs. Fisher and Urey called *Getting to Yes*; if we had it back in my time, there would have been a lot fewer dead Chinese peasant soldiers. And if more of *your* people were trained in its arts, there would be fewer lawyers, judges, and referees needed in the world."

We tell Mr. Sun that we are familiar with the book and its importance in the modern science of conflict resolution. In fact, we have built this section of the problem-solving model around the tenets of the book and do not wish to co-opt concepts that are so beautifully captured in the original. However our model would be incomplete without a discussion of what happens in the unfortunate circumstance, common in the real world as opposed to the world of books and dreams, when things really start to fall apart.

Since we have tried, through the language and teaching of Mr. Usher, to walk a path that is so simple that even a child will not stumble, we suggest to Mr. Sun that we let Mr. Usher and the Children learn about conflict resolution together. We reserve the right, however, at the end of the chapter to proffer some ideas about how we cannot only "get to yes," but how we can "get ahead of no" in the first place.

*   *   *   *

The Lesson of the Fight

Most of the time the students at Mr. Usher's school got along and were happy, but every so often, just like big people do, the children got crosswise with each other. This was just one of those times.

It was a sunny spring day when the begonias were in full bloom and the robin eggs had just hatched, and you could hear the babies chirping hungrily from their nest in the big oak tree. The children were out at recess, playing all around the schoolyard, enjoying the warm day after our long, cold winter. Suddenly a loud shriek split the normal hum of the playground, and nearly all of the children raced across the playground to a spot over by the edge of the grass. They were pushing and jostling and yelling, and in a flash two or three teachers were in among the children, calming them down and telling them to go back to their games. Mr. Usher stood between two boys, each with blood running out of his nose, and both covered with dirt and grass like they'd been rolling around in a barnyard. Mr. Usher had his arms crossed and his face turned sternly downwards.

Schuyler, a smallish, stoutly built boy seemed to have had the worse of the fight. He was sobbing quietly, looking down at his shoes, and trying to get his nose to stop bleeding. Robbie, a big boy from the next grade up, stood with his hands on his hips and looked around the schoolyard, just about anywhere except up at Mr. Usher.

After a few minutes, Mr. Usher put a hand firmly on the boys' shoulders and led them off to Principal Button's office, and that's all anyone knew about The Fight until the next day.

The next morning, the first students to arrive in Mr. Usher's classroom saw a most curious sight. Next to each of their chairs was an extra chair. Soon the Children had all taken off their coats and placed their books in their desks and taken their seats, and all the while Mr. Usher sat quietly watching them from behind his big wooden desk in the front of the class. When they were all quiet, Mr. Usher stood up and, without a word, walked out of the room.

In a minute he was back, followed by Ms. Pell, and behind Ms. Pell, all of the students in Ms. Pell's class, who each took a seat in the extra chairs next to the Children's desks. Soon they were all seated and quiet, all without a word from either teacher. Then, Mr. Usher walked over to Robbie, who was a student in Ms. Pell's class, took him gently by the arm, and had him change places with the student sitting next to Schuyler. Robbie started to argue with Mr. Usher, but stopped in midword when Mr. Usher looked down at him and put his finger up to his lips. Schuyler sat quietly without saying a word, though he edged his chair nervously away from Robbie's.

Mr. Usher went to the front of the room and sat on the edge of his desk, hands on his knees, and looked out over the crowded classroom.

"In my classroom," Mr. Usher began, "we spend a lot of time finding problems and studying problems and understanding problems and solving problems. Mostly these are problems that are just sitting there waiting for someone to come along and ask some good questions and hopefully arrive at a solution. But sometimes problems almost act as if they are alive, as if they don't *want* to be solved. The problem doesn't sit still and give us time to study it and think about it and try different ideas and solutions. Usually that's because this kind of problem involves people. When we have a problem with another person or a group of people, we call that kind of problem a Conflict, and Conflicts can be some of the hardest problems to solve.

"Our two classmates, Schuyler and Robbie, had a conflict yesterday out on the playground, and it ended up with two bloody noses, a trip to Principal Button's office, and some pretty upset and angry parents—not the way any of us would like to start a week, I imagine.

"So we are going to use this unfortunate incident, not to embarrass these two young men, who are probably pretty much as ashamed as they can be already, but to learn some lessons about conflict. This lesson is not about Schuyler and Robbie; it's about all of us who have ever been in a situation, or ever will be, where it seems that a fight is the only solution. And sooner or later that will happen to all of us.

"Now I know this isn't going to be easy," continued Mr. Usher, "but Robbie and Schuyler, please tell us why you were fighting yesterday. And any of the rest of you can help out if you were over there and saw it."

Robbie and Schuyler quickly glanced at each other under their eyelids and just as quickly looked away. Both looked as if they could think of a hundred things they would rather be doing than talking about the fight in front of all their friends. Mr. Usher waited patiently; the only sound in the classroom was the ticking of the big clock on the back wall. Finally Schuyler looked up.

"He and a bunch of his friends wouldn't let us play softball on the corner field. We always play softball there during the second half of recess. They think they own the field or something."

"That's not true!" blurted out Robbie. "We always play dodgeball on the corner field, but we just didn't get out to recess on time yesterday. They wouldn't let us have our game. We asked nicely but they were being real jerks."

With that, the silence was broken and almost every child in both classes seemed to have been part of the tussle on the field, and all were willing to shout out their support of one side or the other, most of which contained the words "jerk" or "bully" or "stubborn" or "nasty" or others that we would expect from two sides that have just seen their two friends in a fist fight. Mr. Usher let them go on for a while and then finally held up his hand for order.

"Thank you all," he began. "I think we have a good idea now of this conflict. Let's start asking some questions and see if there might be a better way to have solved it than trading bloody noses.

"You all seem to feel that the problem is that Robbie and Schuyler and their teammates were being rude or selfish. But I don't think that is really the case at all. Who thinks they see another problem here?"

The children in both classes thought quietly for a few moments, and then Karl, who had been with Mr. Usher for several years, raised his hand.

"The problem is that both groups wanted to use the field at the same time. The nastiness was just the result."

"Very good," said Mr. Usher. "You have just identified the first important step in getting through a tough problem like this one. *Don't confuse the people with the problem itself.* Robbie and Schuyler may not be best buddies all the time, but most of you on both teams get along pretty well every day at recess. Things turned nasty because you could not all use the field when you wanted to. That's the problem. Solve the real problem and the name calling and punches never happen." With that, Mr. Usher took a moment and wrote the problem, just as Karl had stated it, in big letters on the chalkboard.

"Now let us ask another question," continued Mr. Usher. "What would have made both teams happy yesterday?"

Several students from both teams called out that, of course, all they wanted was to use the field. Both teams wanted to play a game at recess; they just wanted to play different games.

"Both teams were so wrapped up in the name calling that you all forgot why you really had a problem in the first place. You both really wanted the same thing: to be able to choose your own game at recess. I would think we could solve a problem where we all want the same thing without resorting to name calling and punches."

Some of the students nodded their agreement, a lot just hung their heads, and Robbie and Schuyler just stared straight ahead.

Karl raised his hand. "But both teams *didn't* want the same thing. They both wanted to play a game, but they are different games."

"True," said Mr. Usher, stroking his chin a bit. "Which is why this is a difficult problem in the first place. And difficult problems take more work to solve. But once we identify the *real* issue, and once we have learned what everyone *really* wants as an outcome, we at least have a chance to get to work."

Mr. Usher went back to the blackboard at the front of the class. "I wrote the problem in big letters on the board for a reason. You are all sitting together, side by side. The problem is up here on the board. If you want to solve a tough problem that involves people without getting into a fight, you have to treat the *problem* as your opponent, not each other. You are all on the same team, and the problem is what you are trying to beat. You all want the same thing: to be able to play the game of your choosing at recess. Now it's time to act like a team, work together instead of at odds, and see if you can beat the problem.

"There are always a lot of ways to beat a problem; our next task is to think of some options and then chose the best one. Not every option will be perfect, but if we don't have any ideas from which to choose, we are stuck. Who can think of a possible solution, even if it is not perfect?"

The students all thought quietly for a few minutes, and then Teresa raised her hand.

"One team could have just given in and walked away," she said. "Maybe they could have played another game."

"Good," said Mr. Usher, writing her thoughts on the chalkboard. "It's not perfect because both teams would not get to play their preferred game, but at least the fight would have been avoided. Any more?"

Matt spoke up. "They could have agreed to play softball and dodgeball on alternate days instead of arguing each day over the field. Neither team would get all of what they want, but at least they would get some of what they want."

Mr. Usher wrote Matt's idea on the board as well, and pretty soon, as more of the students came up with more ideas, the chalkboard was covered with writing. One student suggested they ask Principal Button to make a new softball diamond on the other corner of the grass. Another wondered if they could invent a new game that was half softball and half dodgeball that everyone would like to play every day. A third suggested short games that would each last exactly half of recess. Pretty soon Mr. Usher was down on his knees writing in small letters at the bottom of the board, and chalk dust floated across the front of the room. Finally Mr. Usher stood up, pushed his glasses back up from the end of his nose, and brushed off his hands.

"We are not going to discuss all of these right now and pick one; that is for all of you to do, as a team, if you want to avoid another fight. But now you have a lot of great ideas and if you work hard, I think you can solve this conflict peacefully. In fact, if you had sat down together yesterday, I bet you would have thought up a lot of these on your own, and I doubt there would have been a fight at all."

"But this takes a lot of time," said Robbie. "If we had taken all this time yesterday, there wouldn't have been time to play any game, so none of us would have been happy."

"You are absolutely right, Robbie," said Mr. Usher. "But look at what happened because you were in a rush to solve your problem with your fists. You got in a lot of trouble, we are all sitting here talking about it, and you probably are going to be spending some time grounded at home. So either way, you aren't going to get off easy, and you aren't going to be able to play your game until you spend some time working the problem out. The good part is that when you all work together as a team to beat the problem instead of each other, the problems usually stay solved.

"There are a lot more steps we can learn about working to solve tough problems, but this is enough for one day. The teachers and the principal are not going to solve this problem for you. When you were little kids, your parents or teachers or babysitters acted as judges and told you what to do. It may have kept the noise level down, but it did not teach you how to avoid your own conflicts. You are old enough now not to run to Mommy or Daddy to solve your problems for you. There's only one field out there. If there is another fight today, so be it. But if you want to work together to find a better solution, you know how to start.

"Good luck."

And with that, Mr. Usher and Ms. Pell dismissed their classes to recess. The students did not all walk out together arm in arm and best of friends, and in fact no one played either softball or dodgeball on the field that day. Neither Robbie nor Schuyler seemed to be interested in leading team games that week at all. But some of the other Children must have gotten together and sorted out some ideas and new rules amongst themselves because as long as the Children went to the school there weren't any more fights about softball or dodgeball.

*   *   *   *

Not fair? The problem was too easy, and the Children should have been able to solve it in a heartbeat? This isn't really a problem that should lead to conflict? Insert "Jerusalem" for "corner field" and we see how problems that seem easy can be the toughest to solve.

The *Getting to Yes* model of conflict resolution has egg-like perfection: it is simple, compact, and complete. It gives us the tools to become first-order problem solvers in cases where solutions seem remote or even impossible. It should be taught in every school and every management training seminar. Period.

Just as we asked the question "what comes before problem solving?" and discovered the importance of "problem finding," we now ask, "What comes before conflict resolution?" The obvious answer is *conflict avoidance*. Surely the best, and only surefire way to resolve conflicts is to make sure they never happen in the first place. While even Sun Tzu recognized the dangers of physical conflict and warned against undertaking battle if it could be avoided, the preponderance of his advice presupposes that conflict, either with people, problems, or ourselves, is unavoidable. In some few cases it probably is. In many cases it is not, and if we shift the way we think about or approach conflict, we can learn to not only "get to yes" but also to "get ahead of no."

At the risk of seeming playful, if not arrogant, we will try to use the ancient vernacular.

The soldier is trained to fight, not to sign a treaty.

We are all conditioned to approach conflict combatively. From the youngest age, we are bombarded by our culture through movies, literature, and television to stand up to the bully; our heroes fight in the courtroom, the battlefield, the ball fields, the dusty streets of the Old West. We see horrific fist fights on the screen where the hero comes out with little more than a split lip; legal battles that ignore the cost in time and money to both litigants; wars where physical ground is gained but moral ground is lost. We are not taught to explore options, to form a team with our adversaries, to compromise. We need to recognize this cultural conditioning and opt out of it. To avoid conflict we must first recognize that it is neither inevitable nor good.

Paper can be torn by the weakest child, burned by a single match, ripped by even a casual wind.

Mutual interest and trust, not contracts, build strong relationships that can withstand dissonance. Contracts, agreements, treaties, and prenuptials are all brandished when the parties are already at real odds. In a law-ordered society, legal documents are helpful in resolving conflict but less helpful in avoiding it. Future conflict is avoided by building strong personal relationships that will prevail through the inevitable disagreements. Paper agreements of any ilk should be treated like notes: a good record of what was agreed upon but not the foundation for the agreement itself. The foundation of working relationships must be mutual interest and, if possible, trust.

Wolves are known by their howls in the night; armies raise dust over the horizon; storms are preceded by colored skies and seabirds; smoke blows ahead of fire.

We must learn to see trouble coming from a distance. Real conflict does not brew up and explode overnight. There are always warning signs; if addressed early there is the possibility, if not the guarantee, that escalation can be minimized or avoided. The best way to see the warning signs of conflict is through open and frequent communication. An agreement, a partnership, a marriage, moving in next door to a new neighbor should all prompt an increase in direct communication.

First plan for escape, and then plan for battle. This is not cowardice.

Anyone who has been in combat knows that there are no winners. Whether on the playground, in the courtroom, or on the battlefield, combat extracts a long-term cost from all parties, including the perceived victor. The cost is in the degradation of long-term relationships that could have been profitable had the conflict not escalated. We must retool our training to value the creative problem solver over the reactionary.

There is a time for ambassadors and advisors and a time for them to be sent out of the room.

Don't let third parties control relationships. Generals, parents, lawyers, counselors, and even mediators are trained to resolve conflicts in their own ways. To avoid conflict in the first place requires a first-person relationship that is strong enough to sort out critical issues as they arise. Take advice from your counselors but do the heavy lifting yourself.

If you win and your opponent loses, you still have an enemy.

Conflict will best be avoided if all sides commit to fairness for all sides. Win-win solutions to conflicts are good; balanced relationships based on fairness to all parties will prevent conflict from arising in the first place. The company owner who looks after his employees as well as himself; the coach who recognizes that his student athletes need to be students as well as athletes; the conquering nation that rebuilds its adversary instead of enslaving it; this type of balance will prevent costly trouble in the future.

You should avoid narrow defiles where the only path lies between steep walls and a swift torrent.

There are many pathways to a solution. If we find ourselves with a single option, particularly one that is dangerous, we have probably, if not certainly, made a mistake in the past. We never should have arrived at the point where our options are this limited. In hindsight we can almost always see how options could have been expanded had the parties been more flexible in previous decisions. If we fail to use our tools of brainstorming, compromise, flexibility, and creativity, we find ourselves in the narrow defile where the cost of either success or failure is frequently very high.

*   *   *   *

We find ourselves back in the armory with the menace of midnight creeping somewhere outside the thick, damp walls. It is a heavy, hateful place, and we want to leave. Mr. Sun sits on a low bench, shoulders slumped, mud on his boots, his helmet cast aside, his leather jerkin torn and ripped, as he wipes his hands on a rust-stained rag. He looks up tiredly at us as we enter.

"You're right, of course," he sighs wearily, almost as if he was beyond caring about right or wrong. He bends down to unlace his leggings. "We usually don't try hard enough to avoid conflict. Battle, in whatever form, is a bad option. No one wins. Ever.

"But sometimes we really do try and things just fall apart. We revere our peaceful heroes; we ask questions and solve problems; we use every tool at our disposal, and sometimes it still doesn't work out. Maybe we make a mistake in process or judgment. Maybe we don't have the training or experience we need. And maybe, sometimes, good and bad just leave the column labeled 'subjective' and fall into the realm of objectivity. Sometimes the hostage has a gun to her head and we can take the shot. Sometimes appeasement is both the only option and a recipe for disaster. Sometimes the fanatics attack that fabric of our civilized community that allows us more often than not to turn the other cheek. Sometimes the option of fighting, no matter how horrific, is better than the option of not fighting. It's lousy. It stinks. In many ways, it means that we have failed because we are in that narrow defile and we should have been able to find a better path. There are those who will disagree, who will say that any disagreement, no matter how wide the gulf, can be spanned short of violence. Maybe they are right; we have proven that nothing is impossible, no matter how improbable. Maybe we will all get to that point in the future, and we can lock this room and throw away the key.

"In the meantime," says Mr. Sun, wiping clean the blade of his long single-edge sword and shunting it sharply back into its sheath, "sometimes we have to trash the pretty metaphors and a warrior is just a warrior."

Step 7: Failure and Redemption

What if our fundamental assumptions are false?
Marissa Vernec, Falconer Class of 2004

I have to tell you right now that not all stories of Mr. Usher are blessed with warm rays of sun and flower bouquets. We told you in the Introduction that sometimes we have to fall out of the warm cocoon of our theoretical path, and sometimes that takes us into places of darkness. Mr. Usher would be a blank dream if we did not see, at least this once, that all of us know doubt and even desperation. After all, this is real life.

*   *   *   *

The Lesson of Failure

So it was on a cold February morning, during that time of year when the comforting magic of holly berries and midnight candles have faded to the edge of our memories, when, in the valley, the sun wakes up late and leaves us early, that Michael happened to be the first to school. It was still dark outside, the Big Dipper sharing a black north sky with a million stars like crystals on satin, and Michael's breath puffed out in smoke-signal clouds as he huddled past the old oak tree, scraping clean a dark path across the frosted grass. The door to the school was unlocked of course; even in the bottom of winter, someone at the school is sure to arrive before the first student to turn up the heat and throw on a light against the dark.

Michael hung his heavy coat on its hook in the closet in Mr. Usher's room and moved quietly to his desk. It was not unusual for students to come to school early to finish their homework in the quiet musty warmth of the classroom. Sometimes Mr. Usher would show up also in the dark morning, and they might do their separate work, he at his big desk in front of the class, the students at theirs, or they might chat about something of seeming portent from one of their days.

Michael took out some paper and began to work on an essay that was due later in the week. He wrote and thought and wrote some more, and in thinking about where the essay might go, his eyes wandered randomly to the front of the room to Mr. Usher's big desk, where they lit upon an envelope, half hidden in shadow, taped to the front of the desk. Still thinking about his essay, his eyes thoughtlessly read on the envelope in Mr. Usher's hand, "To Whom it May Concern."

Buried in distant thought, it took a moment to snap in Michael's mind: certainly a strange address and a strange place for Mr. Usher to leave an envelope. He shrugged at the mystery and bent his head back down to his pen and paper.

And this, dear reader, especially you young readers who have proven beyond the pessimism of college deans and business consultants that strategy and wisdom and self-determination are within the gentle grasp of young and old alike, this is where we let go of the façade of cool mountain streams, fresh autumn days under the paternal oak tree, and friendly puffs of chalk-dust sun beams. This is where we grab fictional license and hold it up to the light of expediency, not because we want to or because it is theoretically possible, but because we need to see what happens under pressure. We need to fall down the rabbit hole, even if the story line suffers. So damn the improbability; Mr. Usher needs help.

In one world, Michael would wait and wait; the other students would arrive; the bell would ring cheerily through the halls to announce another day of unbound learning. And after a few minutes of anxious waiting with no teacher, another teacher would come oversee the Children, or Michael would carefully un-tape the envelope and take it to the principal who would read it and then maybe call Mr. Usher at home, or the police, or 911. But we don't need the principal or the police, and neither does Mr. Usher. He needs Mr. Sunny to see the envelope. So here is what we will do.

"To Whom It May Concern." After a few minutes, Michael left his desk, gently un-taped the envelope, and opened it. After all, he certainly was as concerned as anyone else at that point. Sitting back at his desk, he laid flat the two typed pages and read them. Then he re-read them.

How does he know that he must take the letter to Mr. Sunny? How does he even know Sunny exists, tucked away in the forest, sharing stories of ancient battles, cups of tea, and long mushroom hunts with Mr. Usher? Easy. We are all in this together: the Children, Mr. Usher and Sunny, Sun Tzu and the Filipino college students, gravity and sugar, the Falconers of Francis Parker School, you and I. We are all part of the kaleidoscope, and we know each other as each piece of the puzzle knows its neighbors.

So we will all slide past the substitute who taught the Children that day, and the curious angst of all the other teachers when Mr. Usher failed to arrive at school. Michael, knowing what needed to be done, slipped away after school, pulling his heavy winter coat about him, and headed off into the forest in the growing darkness, following deer trails and meadow breaks through thin crusty snow to the small cabin hidden amongst the oak and alder trees.

Michael knocked timidly on the door, the soft tap-tap echoing off the still darkness. When no one answered he knocked harder, his mind flirting with the alarming thought of an empty cabin, nowhere to turn, and then what? But before his panic widened, the door creaked open, and Sunny pushed his head through in his near-sighted mole sort of way, spilling warm light onto his uninvited guest.

"Good evening, young man, and what in the name of all that is good and toasty are you doing here?" he asked, opening the door a bit wider onto the wooden porch.

"You probably don't remember me," Michael replied in his best go-to-visit-grandma voice. "My name is Michael and I am one of Mr. Usher's students, and I think he might be in trouble or need help."

Sunny peered at Michael more closely, pulling his spectacles down off of his forehead. His eyes lit up with recognition.

"Ah, yes, of course!" he exclaimed. "I remember seeing you one day when Mr. Usher had his class studying a square piece of ground at the edge of the forest. And another time when you were all hiking in the mountains and had to divert around some rather large bears. Come in, come in, and get out of that cold."

So Michael squeezed through the porch door, wondering more than a bit how Mr. Sunny could have been in those two spots on those two days without the Children or Mr. Usher seeing him, and he let Sunny take his overcoat and drape it on the back of a threadbare sofa. Sunny motioned for Michael to pull up a thickly padded easy chair in front of the fire as he did so himself, and they both settled down to a back-lit glow of crackling pine logs.

"Now Michael, if Mr. Usher is in trouble or needs help, you should have gone to the principal or the police. I'm sure that Mr. Usher has taught you that there are times of emergency when we have to solve problems quickly, and when someone is in trouble, it may be one of those times."

"I don't think it's that kind of trouble," Michael replied quietly, pulling the envelope out of his shirt pocket and handing it across the hearth to Sunny. "I think you should read this."

Sunny took the envelope, noting the familiar handwriting of his friend and confidant scrawled across the cover. He opened it, took out the two pages, looked over the top of his glasses at Michael, and then held up the paper to the flickering firelight.

This is what he read:

"I'm not who I thought I was. Still meditations on the edge of granite bluffs gathered a dusty powder of neglect; I tried and failed even though the Teacher said it would work. I gave up trying. I wanted God to help only when it was buoyed by ecstatic revelations. When He ignores, I fail; when He helps, I succeed. It's so easy to collapse into this velvet-lined bear trap that snags unpious souls. Struggling against the jaws, they tighten. Failing to struggle, the universe is a desert plane where I can't illuminate dark nights any more than clay pots of dry sage burning.

This isn't Walden, or even a blood-red balcony sunset following a day of bullfights and sangria. That would be too easy, too external, too shallow. The metaphors and lessons don't slice deeply enough, and the edge they leave is artificially hygienic. Imperfection hurts too much, begs the instability of a three-legged stool where one leg is almost worn through. Walden is selfish, but I can't find another setting, another window that is less so.

Somewhere I confused elegance and beauty. A simple slavish devotion to a snow owl's angel-white glide over moonless frosted meadows; two wistful lovers bound in borderless tea ceremony *wa*; the spherical completeness of a glass bead game. Saints and sages promise the possibility, or maybe the inevitability of perfection, even if only in glimpses. Who am I to argue? Gild an artistic puzzle of personal construction, and it is both elegant and beautiful. But what about the pure pain of deconstruction, of standing, toes clenched on the edge of mistake, delusion, misunderstanding, mind and soul grasping at phantom handholds that may never have existed outside of misplaced faith? They weren't all crazy, the anti-saints and anti-sages who fell into the bell jars of despair, unable to selflessly disconnect passionate egos from storm-tossed foam. They saw the fine line between possibility and probability, the same gossamer border between selfless and selfish, but it did not hold the weight.

This is not Walden: the holes are real and just as elegant as the prehistoric light filtering through the trees, illuminating small handles and rungs that lead out of the abyss. They are constants, sometimes well hidden, in a quagmire of treacherous footing. Perfection is at hand, precisely where purgatory meets the colors and sounds of the world: I know it, believe it, and see it. I want to stop the rudderless nights with the unseemly pretence of an insider's tip, with little stones that claim to have been laid as base cobbles or traveler's shrines on the path to redemption.

Gone fishing."

When he was finished, Sunny gently refolded the papers and absentmindedly tucked them under the edge of a book on the end table.

"I must say, young man, I think you have done the right thing bringing this to me, though how and why you decided to do so are a puzzle. But here, I have been a terrible host. You must still be frozen inside. How about a cup of tea or cocoa?"

Michael thanked him and gladly wrapped his hands around a thick mug of steaming hot chocolate, and the two sat close to the now-waning fire. After a minute or two, Sunny coughed nervously.

"Why did you bring this to me, and why do you think Mr. Usher is in trouble?"

"Mr. Usher has always been so sure of himself," Michael began, talking into the fire as if it held the remnant of a half-forgotten dream. "He always seems to know how to solve his problems and is positive and cheery. If he wrote that," he said raising his nose as if to an annoying smell towards the papers on the table, "he is despondent or desperate. It seems that he is at the bottom of a hole and can't find his way out. I don't think the police are the ones to help him with a problem he can't solve."

Mr. Sunny nodded slowly in reply. "I think you are absolutely right," he said, "but I also think you should not worry too much. He may be in a deep hole right now, but he knows too much to stay there for long. It's getting late, and I doubt if your parents would be happy for you to spend a night here. So let's bundle up, and I will walk you back to the edge of town. Leave the rest to me; I am quite sure I shall see Mr. Usher soon, and then we will do our best to set this right."

The two of them gathered their heavy coats about them and marched silently back across the trails and meadows that Michael had followed an hour before. Soon they saw the twinkle of town lights between the trees, and stumbled onto the path behind the school. When they could see the black silhouette of the old oak tree against the lights and stars, Sunny put out his hand and took his leave.

"If you see Mr. Usher, tell him to come see me. Don't worry. Even teachers don't know everything, and maybe Mr. Usher just needs a little class of his own right now."

And with that, the two parted ways, Michael stepping quickly across the frosted playground and then running down the street to his house on the corner. Sunny set a slow pace back through the forest, deep in thought, oblivious to the far-off banshee shriek of a screech owl, the dull cold of the bottomland air, and the mythic fabric of dark, bare trees.

*   *   *   *

The first yellow- green shoots of meadow snow flowers had just snuck through the remnants of winter's white blanket when Mr. Usher paid his long-postponed visit to Sunny. It was a late afternoon, and Sunny was sitting on his front porch, a wool blanket drawn tightly over his legs against the cool springtime breeze. He watched his friend approach through the greening oaks and the budding apple trees.

Wordlessly, Mr. Usher sat in a wicker rocker on the other side of the porch. For a few minutes both watched the forest, waiting for the other to speak. Sometimes there is comfort in the silence between friends. This was not one of those times.

Finally, Sunny broke the silence.

"It's good to see you in one piece. I guess we have some things to talk about."

Mr. Usher nodded, still looking at the blowing trees.

"I am not all of who I thought I was. I've asked all the questions I know to ask and can't find the answers."

Two sparrows chased a noisy crow high in the darkening sky, wheeling in the wind until the dark caw-caw had faded into the forest.

"I read your note," Sunny said quietly, playing with a frayed strand of wool on his blanket. "The fact that you are here means that you are hopeful of seeing your way out of your quandary. Whatever the problem is, I suggest we do our best to give it a fresh look together. And there is no better way to do that than to scrub away whatever is old and come at the problem clean and unburdened. Let's take a long, hot soak."

With that Sunny led Mr. Usher out back of his small house, down a narrow trail through a thick stand of alder trees, to a small wooden hut set against the hillside. Mr. Usher had never seen this hut before, but, like us, he was used to things coming and going around Sunny as needed.

Sunny held open the heavy wooden door to let Mr. Usher pass. Inside, a steaming pool of water swirled gently amongst the rocks, and a bench off to one side held thick white towels, sponges, and a heavy brown earthen jug of cold apple cider. Following Sunny's lead, the two friends set their clothes aside and sank down in the water and steam. For a long time they soaked; they scrubbed themselves pink with the heavy, coarse sponges; and when they felt ready to melt away in the heat, they drank deeply from the cider jug. Finally Sunny said they had had enough; they both wrapped themselves in warm robes and walked weak legged back down the now-dark trail to the house.

When they were settled in front of a crackling fire, a plate of bread and fresh butter and last year's dried fruit between them, Sunny smiled at his friend and began.

"So tell me what happened." The best thing about good friends is they don't have to beat about the bush.

"The specifics aren't important," Mr. Usher began. "I spend my whole life trying to get the Children to set a high bar for themselves, to have the confidence that they can achieve lofty goals, just like their heroes. I try to give them the tools they need to run this race and win, not for me or for their parents or their friends or their legacy, but for themselves. I have always trusted that what I teach them, while not perfect, leads them closer to the truth than where they started. But now I don't know. I did something that I know was wrong. If I failed myself, if we are unable to really craft ourselves beyond what our nature allows, then I have failed the Children as well. What I have taught them, what you have taught me, may only be good up to a point, and after that, when the real challenge comes, when we want to fight some flaw in our nature to ascend to the nature of our heroes, things fall apart. Maybe it's better not to lead at all than to possibly lead towards a false hope."

Sunny held his fingers in a narrow steeple in front of his face and thought a while. "I was pretty sure that was how you would see it," he says. "In fact, I have been pondering this same dilemma myself. When I first wrote *The Art of War* so many years ago, I did not adequately consider the issue of fundamental failure. My advice was black and white, even if it is veiled in a Tao that is mysterious to some: *do this and you are a warrior; fail to do it and you are not a warrior.* I've been bothered by that for a long time. Over the years as I have watched you teach your Children, and as we have discussed our mutual ideas, I have thought we might end up at this place, and so we have. I think I know the answer, but it is getting late and we can talk about it in the morning."

With that, Sunny walked down the hall to his own room, closed the door, and Mr. Usher curled up with a blanket on the deep sofa before the smoldering fire.

*   *   *   *

In the kitchen, Sunny stirs a skillet of fried potatoes and mushrooms; an old-style teapot hisses furiously on the stove; and from deep in the oven, the smell of muffins fills the cabin. Sunny waves Mr. Usher over to the table, and within a few minutes they are both devouring a hearty breakfast. When they are finished, they refill their tea mugs and take their respective wicker chairs on the porch outside. A bright morning sun melts the edges of the last slushy snow in front of the house, and the apple trees seem to have added a double frosting of new white blossoms overnight.

Sunny begins. "Every day you encounter people leading normal lives. They are mothers and fathers, students, co-workers, a waitress in the corner restaurant or a gardener cutting the grass at school. They are putting one foot in front of the other. Doing the best they can. No theorizing, no teaching or preaching, no fairy tales, no gilding. Getting up in the morning and getting done what needs to be done before nightfall. Are these people succeeding or failing? Are they good or bad? Are they right or wrong in how they live their lives? Are they warriors or not?"

"I don't know. I can't see into their pasts or their souls, so I have no idea. I don't think it matters. They are who they are, and any judgment of mine would be pointless at best."

"What do you think these people are seeking?" Sunny asks. "Do they have a shared set of goals and ambitions? Are their predicaments random or predictable? How do they fit into our model?"

Mr. Usher sets his coffee cup down on the end table and lets his gaze fall out the window into the forest. "I have no reason to think or believe that they are seeking anything other than the degree of happiness or satisfaction that is common to all of us."

"If such a simple desire is common to all of us, including you, why have you reached a point of despondency?"

"It must be selfishness and ego. What else could allow me to believe that I am immune to the traumas of others, that a theoretical model, in the hands of anyone with imperfection, is perfect?"

"What is it that you want that you have failed to attain?"

"Clarity. A unified theory. The sense that, after a full life of trying, I got it right."

"To truly consider yourself a warrior," says Sunny, "you must set your personal bar very high. If the challenges are not great enough, you either must raise the bar, or cease to consider yourself a true warrior. Guaranteed success means you have set the bar too low. Things like clarity and a unified theory … I would say those are fairly high bars.

"At some point, you are going to fail, not at a simple task or at solving a problem. You are going to fail in your fundamental goals, your belief system, your moral foundation, or your self-view. It is an inevitable result of setting the bar higher and higher.

"But failure, as you have taught your Children, is inevitable in your own model. You cannot be more perfect than the people you encounter every day. You may be able to set higher philosophical goals or more complex personal challenges, but you cannot escape failure.

"So for your model to be complete, there must be a last step, one that recognizes the inevitability of failure and allows us to move on towards our goal of happiness. The question is, for you, how can you overcome this feeling of failure? What will allow you to step back into the ring and try again?"

Mr. Usher gazes deeply at his friend without blinking. Sunny has never seen him this intent.

"If I knew the answer to that, I would not be in this funk."

"I will answer it for you then," says Sunny. "You need to know that you have both the right and the responsibility to try again. This is your redemption. This is the warrior's redemption: another chance; the chance to be wrong in what we do, but right in the passion with which we try. It is not the Christian redemption, or the beggar's or the orphan's; we cannot saddle them with either the promise or the limitations of our destiny, nor can they do so with us.

"So I have a postulate that I will offer, and I could kick myself that I did not finish *The Art of War* with it all those years ago:

Redemption comes from trying, despite the sure knowledge that you will fail.

"Please be careful to note that I use the word 'will' and not 'might' to qualify the certainty of failure. If you are a warrior, a true leader, a falconer, a teacher, you *must* fail, or you have not set the bar high enough. Your redemption is that you will keep trying anyway, despite this sure knowledge. Most of our heroes fail in the end: they crash their plane, fail to feed or free their people, die on the last assault of the mountain, or succumb to the imperfection of their humanity. But they are redeemed in our eyes and in our faith because they tried, they gave us a ring to grasp, a height to which we might aspire.

"Only God, through perfection, escapes this dilemma. And at least right now, you and I are not God. But in the eyes of God, and in our own eyes, we can be redeemed if we just don't give up. Some people confess their sins or beg for forgiveness. Some have been promised redemption from their faith in a God that wants only that confession. Others just try to do better next time. We don't know or try to guess if this is right or wrong. Despite our reluctance to do so, we have to forgive ourselves our failures, and get ready to try and fail again. Anything less is the triumph of selfish ego, and we cannot pretend to the title of warrior."

"How do I know if I am trying hard enough, if I am not fooling myself with the illusion of honest effort?" asks Mr. Usher.

"I will answer that question with a question. 'Is gravity a concept or a principle?' Remind yourself of the answer to that *koan* over which you struggled so long, and I think you will find it applies here as well."

Mr. Usher turns his eyes to the window and gazes back across miles and years to remember his answer about the nature of gravity.

"Gravity exists as the natural force between any two bodies. If the bodies are large, the attraction between them can be quantified. If the bodies are extremely small, the Heisenberg Uncertainty Principle comes into play, and we cannot be definitive about the motion of the bodies, and therefore we cannot say with certainty what effect gravity has upon them.

"I define the term 'concept' as being subjective in nature, something that is not proven and repeatable in all cases. I define the term 'principle' in this case to suggest that it is a fundamental repeatable truth upon which we can base predictable and objective observations.

"According to these definitions, and with the problem of the Uncertainty Principle acting on small bodies, we must reject the option that gravity is a principle: it may not apply in all cases.

"Similarly, however, we cannot say that gravity does *not* hold in every case; therefore we must reject the option that gravity is only a concept, subject to our own view of the physical world. It may in fact operate on all bodies with equal elegance; we just can't know.

"We could say that we do not have enough information and therefore the answer is 'I don't know.' I find this inelegant because it smacks of defeatism.

"So the answer is 'Maybe yes or maybe no.' I believe there *is* a definitive answer, but I cannot obtain it within the confines of the physical universe and my own limitations of consciousness. There is a likelihood that I will have a better answer when I am dead and not bound by these limitations."

"I agree," says Sunny, with a warm smile and nodding head. "We cannot know if we have tried hard enough as long as we are bound by our ego and the shadow it casts on the world around us. Such knowledge will come only with the elimination of this self; a few do so through a dedicated life of meditation and removal from the constraints of this temporal universe. Most leave their ego behind with the transition we call death, at which point they will no doubt enjoy a Godly understanding of what has happened and what is yet to happen, and what is merely illusion.

"In the meantime, let's have some more tea."

*   *   *   *

Late in the day, Sunny and Mr. Usher walked back through the forest, enjoying the quiet of late sunlight filtering through the trees and the occasional scamper of a fidgety squirrel through the ground litter.

"Once I sat and watched at the mouth of a great river where it entered an open and windward ocean," said Sunny, as they shook hands and said their good-byes. "Over many years the river had built up a sturdy sandbar that stood up to a tumultuous barrage of waves. The great rolling storm-fed breakers would charge in their lines from the horizon and peak and thunder down on the outer side of the bar and blow spume and froth high into the air. At high tide the sandbar would be nearly submerged, waves racing up the beachfront on one side and the river flooding with the tide on the other.

"Right now you remind me of that sandbar. You have a sturdy foundation that has been built layer by layer and survived over time, but just now the tide and surf are overwhelming you. Just wait, give it some time. The tide will fall and the river always has more sand to add. And despite its ferocity, the cleansing high tide leaves the sandbar less cluttered with driftwood and detritus and noisy seabirds as it recedes."

The two friends shook hands, Sunny turned back to the path into the woods and Mr. Usher walked, hands in his pockets, towards his classroom.

Step 8: The Art of Falconing

Why am I Falconing today? Because it is Wednesday!
Sarah Israel, Falconer Class of 2001

We have returned to that ancient, cold, fog-laden meadow where our path began, and again there are three riders. Mr. Sun sits easily on a tall chestnut mare, looking as comfortable in his ancient hunting costume as he might have a couple of millennia ago. My old dark war pony lumbers doggedly in the mare's footsteps; I am not a horseman. I don't know the third rider by sight, but it must be you, dear reader; who else could it be? You look sleepy and a bit cold, but thermal underwear and hot coffee won't make it to this part of the world for more than two thousand years. You don't have a speaking part in this chapter, but we would not be here without you.

Our horses break through the line of trees on the same path we watched many pages ago. The treetops are mere ghosts in the gently stirring fog that veils us from the surrounding world. We dismount and tie our horses to a tree. Mr. Sun strokes his falcon gently, and we walk together to the center of the meadow. We are at the center of a fuzzy sphere of grass and mist.

"It looks like this is a relatively short chapter," Mr. Sun says, reaching into a leather pouch tied to his belt and offering a small raw treat to his bird. "You decided not to bring your Mr. Usher and his class out with us today?"

"Too many people, too much noise. Might limit our options if we really want to hunt today," I respond. In truth, I just wanted some time alone with Mr. Sun (and our reader of course) to discuss our respective metaphors before we have to part ways.

On Mr. Sun's wrist the falcon sits, blindfold in place, its head cocking back and forth to sounds we can't hear. It ruffles out its chest feathers as if annoyed or anxious to get about its business.

"Why, then, do you use the metaphor of a falconer?" Mr. Sun asks.

"Long before I read your book," I began, "the image came to me of an individual alone, in the center of an experiential sphere, much as we are this morning, skilled in the management and direction of his problem-solving resources, not because he was born skilled, but because he has worked at it. The nature and the type of resources did not matter. What mattered was that the individual had been taught well, that he was prepared; that he sought and found problems passionately; that he was rigorous in his method; that he developed his skills to be strong and precise. I have never used real birds to hunt real prey, so perhaps the metaphor was presumptuous, and I apologize in advance to all real falconers and their birds. But the image seems to have worked with my own students. Each year on the first day of class, unprompted, one or more will ask me 'Why do you call this class The Falconer?' I tell them that we will discuss it at the end, not at the beginning. They grumble. But when the course is almost over, we discuss the imagery, and they always agree that the image fits, and that it was right to leave the explanation until the end."

"In this metaphor, then, what are the falcons?" asks Mr. Sun.

"They are all of our skills and resources that we have developed and trained. Not just the specific method of problem solving, but all of the knowledge and character that we were born with and learn over the years. We have worked and coached these skills until they are ready when we need them. Hopefully we have many falcons ready to fly whenever and wherever the need arises."

"And what are the pigeons or other unfortunate birds which your metaphorical raptors will seek and kill?" asks Mr. Sun.

"They are the problems and opportunities that we seek out and engage in order to lead a full and productive and happy life. In real falconing, the desired result is a dead bird, or maybe just a day alone on a windy plain. In our metaphor, the desired result is an elegant solution to a difficult problem, an opportunity realized, a thought created."

"How would you describe the responsibilities and attributes of your falconer?" Mr. Sun asks.

"The first is *patience*. It takes a long time to learn, develop, and hone strategic skills. Our nature is always to react, but a falconer is nothing without well-trained birds. Falconers can't fly.

"The next is *vision*. We need to know where we are going. The birds do what they are trained to do once they are pointed in the right direction, in the right meadow, at the right time.

"The next is *leadership*. Leadership is earned through a combination of confidence and success. We should welcome the role of leader if we are confident that we have prepared ourselves as well as we can. If we are good leaders, the falcons will cooperate willingly. If they are not willing, it is the leader who is at fault.

"The next is *accountability*. If we claim to have developed our skills, if we purport to lead with confidence and vision, we have the responsibility to apply ourselves as rigorously as possible. We may not succeed every time, but at least we must learn and refine from every experience. We try to get better."

"At the outset of this book," says Mr. Sun, "you suggested some questions that a falconer might ask, some specific guides he might apply to his use of strategy. Might we review these and others in terms of your metaphor?"

"Happily," I reply.

"Should birds be flown in mist or only when they can see their prey clearly? The falconer must judge when and how to use his skills, and whether or not he has the luxury of waiting. In order to make this determination, he must know himself, his falcons, his prey, and his urgency.

"Can more than one bird be flown at once? The falconer must know his own abilities and their limits. 'Multitasking' is an over-used phrase. How many *real* problems can we *effectively* tackle at once?

"What if wild falcons interrupt the hunt? Are we prepared for the inevitability of the unpredictable? Murphy's Law has a new name, Chaos Theory, but they mean the same thing: something unknown always happens. Are we prepared for it?

"What is the nature of the prey? Is it abundant or elusive? The falconer must be confident that he truly knows the nature of his challenge before he lets the birds go. Otherwise he is responsible for wasting precious resources.

"Does the pigeon need to die today? The falconer must decide if it really is a problem that needs attention. We all have limited resources: time, skill, money, knowledge, and patience. As all parents know, we need to carefully decide what battles we will fight with our children and which are not worth fighting.

"Are the falcons in good condition? The application of strategy, like any other skill, requires practice. We can't expect the birds to perform their task well if we have let them sit in the hutch while their wings atrophy."

By now the fog has lifted off of the treetops, and just as in the introduction, a gentle breeze is blowing the mist away like thin smoke from a damp fire. The sun will win its morning battle within the hour, and we think it will be a magnificent day to fly metaphorical birds, let alone the patient, but tightly wound raptor that still clings to Mr. Sun's wrist. I haven't been paying attention but suspect that he has been sneaking the noble bird a wealth of treats in order to buy its relative serenity.

"It seems," says Mr. Sun, "that there are many similarities between your falconers and my generals. We both have come to the conclusion that tactics are important, but they will not be successful unless those wielding them possess certain traits."

"I completely agree," I respond. "While reading and interpreting your *Art of War*, it was clear that you reserved a lion's share of your advice not for 'how' to implement strategy, but for 'whom' the leader needs to be. This is precisely why I believe that we need to introduce these skills and this training, overtly, at an early age. Why hide that which is most important, hoping that somehow, through osmosis, the skills will be learned? I would suggest a summary line for your book that uses your own imagery:

Tactics win battles; generals win wars.

"Well put," says Mr. Sun. "Perhaps the corollary in terms of your metaphor would be

Falcons kill birds; falconers bring home the dinner.

"Exactly, though I hope my vegetarian friends do not take this too literally," I respond.

Since it appears that it will be a few more minutes before the fog lifts, Mr. Sun agrees to review some of Sun Tzu's messages that seem particularly relevant. We agree that there are many passages in the *Art of War* that deal with the nature of leadership, and we will contemplate only a few of our favorites.

Sun Tzu says: *To ensure that your whole host may withstand the brunt of the enemy's attack and remain unshaken—this is effected by maneuvers direct and indirect.*

This means that the skills of problem solving are in two categories: those that can be learned and those of instinct. The true leader will follow teachings and learn methods, but does not ignore his instincts.

Sun Tzu says: *That the impact of your army may be like a grindstone dashed against an egg—this is effected by the science of weak points and strong.*

This means that aggressive pursuit of an answer without the distractions of passion is an example of fullness and emptiness. Confidence without gloating is an example of fullness and emptiness. Desire to achieve and detachment in the face of failure is an example of fullness and emptiness. We are aggressive, yet know that we must live with the results.

Sun Tzu says: *No ruler should put his troops in the field merely to gratify his own spleen; no general should fight a battle simply out of pique. Anger may in time change to gladness; vexation may be succeeded by content. But a kingdom that has once been destroyed can never come again into being; nor can the dead ever be brought back to life. Hence the enlightened ruler is heedful, and the good general full of caution. This is the way to keep a country at peace and an army intact.*

This means that the visionary acts out of rational planning and conception, not out of emotion. Your time and resources are too valuable to waste on unproductive conflict or pursuit of problems that have no solutions. Martyrs cannot fight another day. Pick your major challenges carefully, and you will be in greater control of your life and direction.

Sun Tzu says: *The clever combatant looks to the effect of combined energy, and does not require too much from individuals. Hence his ability to pick out the right men and utilize combined energy. When he utilizes combined energy, his fighting men become as it were like unto rolling logs or stones.*

This means that a leader has the vision and insight to know how and when to apply his resources with the least effort. He does not try to fit a square peg into a round hole if there is a way to make the pegs fit. He makes certain that his skills and resources are ready, so that they may be brought to bear when a problem or challenge arises.

Sun Tzu says: *If equally matched, we can offer battle; if slightly inferior in numbers, we can avoid the enemy; if quite unequal in every way, we can flee from him.*

This means that the leader, using his vision, patience, and insight, knows when to pursue a challenge and when to walk away. There are problems we cannot or do not want to solve.

Sun Tzu says: *With this loss of substance and exhaustion of strength, the homes of the people will be stripped bare, and three-tenths of their income will be dissipated.*

This means that resources are not without limit, regardless of our desire or passion. We must balance our desire to constantly achieve success with our ability to sustain our nature. It is not within our power to solve every problem.

Sun Tzu says: *Thus the skillful general conducts his army just as though he were leading a single man by the hand.*

This means that the successful leader will weave his many resources into a single cooperative force so they are working supportively. Instead of managing many, then, he needs to master only one.

We could go on all morning, but the mist has nearly dissolved before the glorious winter sun, and our host tells us that it is almost time to stop talking and let the bird fly. Mr. Sun folds his arms and scuffs his toe across the damp ground.

"I have a final question," he says. "In your model, and particularly in the lessons that your friend Mr. Usher has taught the Children, we have learned that it is vital to revisit foundational assumptions, to question that upon which we base and derive all of our other wisdom. Your preface begins with an astute declaration that suggests that even *success* is not as valuable a goal as *happiness*. All that we and Mr. Usher and the Children and Sunny have discussed seems to logically follow from the foundational premise that your model can lead to more success and, more importantly, more happiness. But are we not required to reassess that initial statement and question its veracity? What if the original premise is false? Does all that follows collapse?"

"That is an excellent question," I respond (and here I am speaking alone since you, reader, have been silent during all of this chapter), "and we cannot conclude our model with any degree of confidence without addressing it. If it were a fundamentally sound premise, one would expect that it would hold true as much in your ancient time as it would today. We hope that truths and first premises transcend time and place. So let me ask you a question by which we may pursue your line of inquiry.

"We have agreed that, while *The Art of War* has far wider application than merely as an instruction into armed conflict, you in fact earned a good deal of your daily bread as a consultant to the warlords of ancient China. You advised them to think and act strategically in their pursuit of violent victory. Presumably when they followed your advice, they tended to win battles. Did this result make them happier?"

Mr. Sun reflects for a moment. "Yes, I would say that, while warlords tend to be a testy and spoiled lot who are hard to please, in general winning made them happier than losing."

"And what of those who were vanquished?" I ask. "Regardless of whether or not they followed your advice, they lost a battle or a war, or maybe their families and friends and lands. How do you think *they* felt?"

"No doubt," says Mr. Sun, "they felt less happy with their loss."

"So we can conclude," I continue, "that the use of our model may tend to increase our own possibility of a happy life, but it does not follow that it *necessarily* increases overall happiness in the world. It may, in fact, decrease happiness amongst those who are remote to us or whose objectives and goals are in conflict with our own. This brings us to a fundamental question that many of my bright students asked during the years of our seminar instruction. It is a question that is actually far more important even than 'why' and 'what if.' The question is 'who cares?'

"Who cares if I, as an individual, or you, or your general-warlord, or a group of children are happier? Is not the pursuit of happiness through this strategic model just another form of ultimate selfishness? Many of my students asked the question this way: 'Okay, so you and I are more successful and happy, but what about the rest of the world? How and why should I be happy if it does not make the world a better place? Is the world a better place because of my happiness? Will there be fewer wars or genocides, less deforestation, healthier babies, less starvation, more generosity, less greed, greater piety, less despair? We care about all of these things! Shouldn't we be more concerned about them than about our own happiness? Shouldn't the first premise of your model be "At the end of the day, we all want the same thing: a happier, better, more peaceful, loving, and tolerant world in which to live and to leave to future generations"?'"

Mr. Sun nods in agreement. "Yes, you and I both focus our models and practices on the practices of the individual or of a collective like an army that has a single shared goal, not on the effects those practices might have on the larger world. We hope that a person following this path will make correct decisions that result in a net positive outcome, but it is not always so. Genghis Khan and Adolph Hitler were both brilliant students of strategy, up to a point. So how do we reconcile the selfish nature of your first premise with your students' desire to positively affect the world around them?"

"It is a harsh reconciliation," I reply, "and many will find that it reeks of defeatism. But I am a scientist. While I may view my *own* relationship to the external world in a subjective fashion, I do not have the right to force that subjective view on the world itself. I must look at the facts, and the absolutely unalterable fact is this: *the world just doesn't care.*

"We have to understand that, as humans, we have a uniquely superior and self-centered view of our place in the universe. Regardless of whether we believe in creationism or evolution, we believe that we are the most highly evolved species living on a special rock that orbits a special star, and that we live and read and discuss philosophy at a special time, either following the culmination of billions of years of evolution or on a God-produced stage in which we live out our divinely created destinies. We may not believe that we are alone in this regard in the whole universe, but we think we are alone in this regard in this world.

"The problem is that it is all about 'us.' When we say we want the world to be a better place, what we generally mean is that we want people and large mammals to be happier or less distressed as a whole during their lives in this world. A few of us extend this to other sentient species or a longer time frame, but for the majority of us, it is a pretty tightly focused concern relative to the whole world. We view the world through the unique lens of our own humanness.

"But the world is a complex geologic-biologic-hydrologic-cosmologic entity within which we are just a flash in the pan. Let's take this argument to the extreme to see if, in fact, the world cares. Let's do everything really wrong. Let's reject the model of the pursuit of happiness completely; let's do everything contrary to the characteristics of the heroes that we admire. We will be as unthinking, mean-spirited, reactive, devil-may-care as we possibly can. Let's seek maximum unhappiness within the terms of my students' utopia and see if the world cares. We will spurn every friend, burn every forest, dam every river, pollute every lake, kill off half of the species of higher plants and animals, legalize rape and murder, melt the ice caps, escalate war in every corner, spread Ebola, and let fly the nukes. How's that? As bad as it can get? What is the world's view at that point?

"The world in that state is still a geologic-biologic-hydrologic-cosmologic entity. Rain, however acidic, still falls; life, however decimated in diversity and number, still follows the laws of genetics; rivers still carry silt to the ocean; tectonic plates still grind their slow march across the fluid mantle; and the sun still rises and sets. In a time that is vanishingly short from the earth's point of view, let alone that of the entire universe or of God, new species have evolved to fill every environmental niche, viruses have died out and new ones have taken their place, the radiation has dropped to background levels, the atmosphere and hydrosphere have cleansed themselves through natural chemical processes, and the most destructive species in the history of the world, us, is gone, leaving the earth to carry on just as it did for four and a half billion years before 'we' showed up. If we are creationists, we believe that Armageddon or the End of Time has come and gone and it is now up to God to determine how, or if, there is a future for the world.

"I used to put it this way to my students who viewed the Glen Canyon Dam as a metaphor of loss to all who cherish the world's places of beauty that have fallen to the march of human-kind: *just wait for five or ten thousand years.* There is not a scientist alive who actually believes that the Glen Canyon Dam will still be standing, holding back the great waters of the Colorado River, in ten thousand years. In that time period, regardless of what you or I do, the earth will have had another ice age or two, sea level will have risen and dropped a few hundred feet, thousands of species will have become marginalized or extinct, and others will be on their way to claiming their own spot in the march of life. In other words, the world will be largely the same, except from 'our' point of view. And that's just ten thousand years."

Mr. Sun has been listening as we have derived this argument. "Is that not a terribly negative analysis?" he asks. "Even in my time, when life was generally far harsher than it is today, we tried to do things that would tend to make the world around us a better place. Even the warlords, though it might well be contested by a modern democratic standard, pretty much thought that what they were doing was for the greater good, at least as far as their vision could determine it. Rather than giving up, should we not continue to strive towards the goals of our heroes?"

"*Absolutely*," I answer. "But for the right reasons and with our eyes wide open. We have to admit that we are doing it for our own benefit, so that we and those close to us, be they friends, family, elephants, or blue whales, will lead happier, more fulfilled lives. We are happier if we are making the world a better place, and that is more than just okay; it is a lofty goal worthy of a hero. Some of us, those who we see as more generous or compassionate or who just have greater resources, may spread the happiness more widely, and from that spreading they will derive personal satisfaction and happiness. This is as true for our heroes as it is for the rest of us.

"Will any of us ever make the world a significantly better place? I certainly hope and expect so. Will any of us ever save the world? I doubt it, and to even contemplate this degree of effect that we as individuals or groups can have on the entire future of the world is probably preposterous, and certainly egocentric. Thus our first premise is both honest and accurate. The answer to 'Who cares?' is 'We do.' Our model of heroes and warriors and all of what we have developed is valid, not because the world will be better for it, but because *we* will be better for it. I think the resulting postulate in this regard is *Do the best you can because you can. You may not save the world, but you will be happier, and so will those you care about.*"

The bird is now beating its wings restlessly, and the sun has warmed away the last of the morning mist. It is time for action to replace all of the morning's words. Since this is his sport and not ours, we bid Mr. Sun a good day and a good hunt, climb back into our saddles, and ride back down the forest path with the screaming of the flying falcon echoing behind us.

Step 9: Creational Thinking

Human existence can be described as the search for unity within ourselves.
Zoe Landers, Falconer Class of 1998

There comes a time to pull it all together. The weaver sets her warp and weft and creates a unique rug with a pattern that has never been gazed upon since the dawn of time. The painter mixes colors and tints and spreads his vision with a set of well-kept brushes. The scientist turns over an unturned stone, the explorer finds an unknown cave, the athlete runs faster and throws farther, and the orator mines the passion of his very soul and brings his audience to its feet in tears. The mother raises her children, and the children find meaning in a turbulent world. The writer transforms four dimensions into two.

How? They have all learned their separate crafts; they have all practiced with their tools. They learned "how" and "why" and some, the ones who we will study or remember or emulate as heroes, will add some singular spark of insight or introspection, some glimmer that no one else has ever glimpsed in exactly that same way. They will create something unique, new, and wonderful where before there were just pieces and ideas, and then all of the miles on the path will have been worth every step. They will have become who they wanted to be, and they will have shared that victory with the rest of us.

A number of forward-looking educators, researchers, and authors have articulated the vision that, in the future, success will be more closely aligned with the ability to pull together information from disparate sources than with an ability to analyze knowledge from within a single discipline. Daniel Pink's *A Whole New Mind* argues that the last century belonged to the analytical left brainers who designed information and accounting systems and advanced the twentieth century sciences of chemistry and physics. He forecasts that the next century, particularly in developed countries that will be consistently underbid in labor costs for work that is heavy on analysis or repetition, will be marked by those who can effectively bridge the gap between the creative right brain and the analytical left brain. In *Five Minds for the Future*, Howard Gardner provides an excellent outline of the importance of educating for synthesis at the high school level. He portrays the synthesizing mind as one capable of putting information together in new ways for new applications that make sense both to the creator and to a wider audience. Sometimes risk is involved, and creative people may share traits of temperament that allow them to faithfully take such risks. As Gardner states "The creating mind breaks new ground. It puts forth new ideas, poses unfamiliar questions, conjures up fresh ways of thinking, arrives at unexpected answers."

Many of the Children's heroes would reflect these same traits. Crossover sciences like biochemistry and artificial intelligence that will be the hallmark of the twenty-first century require individuals who are both rigorous in their management of knowledge *and* innovative in its creation. Unfortunately, our educational and training systems are still rooted in single discipline mode. The best education today teaches multidisciplinary knowledge, and that is a huge step in the right direction. The real leap will be when we overtly teach our students and employees *how* to be creative, *how* to bridge the gap between the left and right brains, *how* to synthesize data, *how* to use risk as a strength and not a weakness, *where* to look for the gaps that will lead to the new discoveries and innovations and designs that have always been the high watermarks of human development. These are the intellectual tools that are demanded by the world ahead.

*   *   *   *

The Lesson of the Game

Even in stories, children grow older. The Children in Mr. Usher's class were no exception, which is certainly a blessing since they would surely have grown bored learning the same things year after year. When Mr. Usher first came to the school in the valley, the Children were in fourth grade, nine or ten years old, and what he taught them then were things that a nine or ten year old with a bit of guidance and patience might understand and use in his or her daily life. By the time they ventured out into the forest to study the system of a square meter of nature, the Children were eleven or twelve and ready to delve into the real world of analysis. And of course they were strong and independent, if a bit headstrong, young teenagers during the summer of the fated camping trip; Mr. Usher would hardly have tried to shepherd a group of fourth graders through the mountains and past a family of restless bears.

Since we are nearing the end of our time together, it is also time for the Children to be on their way, past the sphere of Mr. Usher and into their own lives.

So it was one late autumn morning in the last year of the Children's schooling that some of the other teachers watched from a distance as Mr. Usher, alone in the outdoor amphitheater, stood in the middle of the stage, arms outstretched, turning slowly as if in a silent, slow motion ballet. He pointed here and there, waved his hands at this corner and that one, framed something invisible with his arms, and then, seemingly satisfied with what only he could see, nodded his head and smiled.

"We're going to play a game," he muttered to the empty benches. "This will do just fine."

That morning in class as the Children settled into their seats, Mr. Usher went to his place at the front of the room and asked for their attention. As with all young men and women at this age, there was a lot of important chatter about clothes and dates for the dance and who had said what to whom yesterday at lunch, but gradually the Children settled into their seats and turned their attention to the teacher.

"The first day I met you," Mr. Usher began, "when you were no more than this big," holding out his arm just a few feet off the floor, " you all told me who some of your heroes were and why. It was a marvelous list of people and characteristics. Over the years we have learned some important tools that will help you in your goal to be more like your own heroes. But there is one more attribute to which we can aspire, a skill that some of your heroes would be surprised to know they had. It will be what we work on this year. It is the skill of Creation.

"One of the main reasons we respect these heroes is that, with or without knowing it, they help us to see things in a new and sometimes completely unique way. They create for us an understanding that did not previously exist. They are, in their own fashion, inventors. They invent understanding, knowledge, and, in many cases, wisdom.

"It is easy to test this. Think of one of your personal heroes and ask the question 'would I see the world in a different way had I never known or heard about this person?' If the answer is yes, then for you that person has created a unique piece of knowledge or perspective.

"As I said, some of our heroes do this without knowing or planning it. But we have taken a purposeful approach in our skills development over the years, and this final step should be no less conscious than all the others. This skill is the most abstract and the most difficult for you to understand, but if you grasp its meaning, you too will become an inventor of knowledge."

There had been many times over the years when Mr. Usher spoke to the Children and the blank looks on their faces were a patient and respectful way to let him know that they had *absolutely no idea* what he was talking about. This was one of those times. A few students looked at each other knowingly as if to say "he's finally lost his mind." Most sat patiently and waited for him to continue.

Kyle, a tall young man who had always prided himself on speaking directly with Mr. Usher, raised his hand. "I have a question," Kyle said.

"I thought and hoped you might," said Mr. Usher.

"We have no idea what you are talking about," Kyle said politely.

"Kyle, that is a statement, not a question, so I cannot respond. We know how important it is to ask questions first and save the statements for later," Mr. Usher replied.

"Sorry," Kyle said. "What are you talking about?"

"That's better," said Mr. Usher. "First let me repeat. The skill we are going to learn is an abstract concept that is difficult to grasp, but we are going to make it less complicated by *experiencing* the skill, not learning about it. You will not 'get it' until the end. It's like baking cookies. You start with a batch of ingredients that independently don't look and taste very good, and certainly don't look like they will end up forming cookies. It's not until you have combined them in a very specific way that they become delicious. That's what we are going to do. We are going to try to create a new recipe for a new metaphorical cookie. But until it is metaphorically baked, even we won't know if the recipe worked or not. If it does work, we have created knowledge or understanding in a new way. If it fails, at least we will have tried, and we will know one more way not to fail next time.

"You will have a lot of questions, and so will I. This is our last project together, and in this we are all students and we are all teachers. So let's get started.

"Over the years we have learned about many great thinkers and writers. Sometimes we have found that they provided great insight, but in a way that perhaps was difficult for people to understand. It's a shame that this should be so; wisdom should be as accessible as possible.

"One of these great thinkers and writers was Herman Hesse. Many years ago he wrote a book entitled *Magister Ludi*. It is a supremely rich story with enormous depth of thought, and we won't try to unravel all of his ideas, but one. In his story his characters create and play a rather remarkable game once each year. He calls it the Glass Bead Game. The object of the game is to combine knowledge in a new and unique way, and then share that knowledge with an audience in a fashion that they can understand, and thereby benefit from its creation. At its best, the Game should incorporate and connect information from diverse fields of our shared experience. For example a game master might relate musical harmonies to a mathematical formula, and then apply that formula to the trajectories of stars. Or he might juxtapose quantum mechanics and Eastern philosophy. She might take the echoes of earthquakes, filter them according to their frequency content, and create earth music. He might study the relationship between the reincarnation of souls and the recycling of the earth's crust.

"I know all of these sound wild, but so would the concept of a cell phone to Daniel Boone.

"We are going to create the Game and present it to the entire school this spring. We may come out looking like champions or fools, but either way we will know more about how new knowledge is created than if we don't try. What do you think?"

It was a credit to the years that Mr. Usher and the Children had spent together that the blank stares, still evident around the room, started to melt. There was a murmur here and there of "I guess so" and "Might as well try," along with a lot of "I don't get it" and "Hmmm."

"This Game will take some time to create," Mr. Usher continued. "We can't expect to create something out of nothing overnight. And we will need to use all the tools we have learned so far in order to hope for success. As a group we will need a single topic to work on and then bring all of our combined experience to bear. As a trial I am going to suggest a topic, and we will see if it is Game-worthy or not. The topic is 'One.'"

"What kind of topic is 'One'?" asked Kyle. "It's just a number."

"We'll see," said Mr. Usher. "Let's brainstorm the topic and see where it takes us. You talk; I'll write."

The Children were well acquainted with brainstorming, as they practiced over the years. But how do you brainstorm a number?

"Well, put up the numeral '1' I guess," said Casey. "That's a start."

"And the written word 'one,'" said Max.

"And the Roman numeral 'I,'" said Aaron, who always was looking for a way to work the ancient classics into any discussion.

"Remember that the most important part of the Game is to combine information from many different areas of thought," Mr. Usher reminded them. "Mathematics is just one area. Think broadly."

So all that morning the Children and Mr. Usher listed thoughts and ideas and images that dealt with the concept "One." They modified their working concept to include the concept "unity." They left the list on the board overnight and added to it the next day and the next. They added some and crossed some off, and finally, tired to death of thinking about "one" and "unity," they all agreed that their brainstorm list was long enough.

And here it is (in fact this list was developed in just under thirty minutes by the first Falconer class at Francis Parker School in 1998):

One
Gold standard
1
$\sin^2 + \cos^2$
y=x
$\sqrt{1}$

1^2

1^n

$$\frac{n}{n}$$

unit circle

$x^2+y^2=1$

$n-(n-1)=1$

$-(-1)$

-1^2

Twenty-six letters in an alphabet

Trinity

United States

Fertilization

Vulcan mind meld

Athletic team

E pluribus unum

Lord of the Rings

Collective unconscious

Labor unions

NATO

Yin-yang

Marriage

OM

Gaiea

Universe

Unified field theory

It was indeed an impressive list (even if some of the items required a mental stretch to link directly to the concept of "Oneness," but that is allowed in brainstorming), and when Mr. Usher reminded the Children how they had initially been stumped with what to say about the concept "One," they all laughed and gave themselves a well-deserved pat on the back.

After a day or so to let the list settle in their minds, Mr. Usher gathered the Children around the front of the classroom.

"Now comes the hard part," he started, at which more than half the class let out an audible groan. "Now we have to create something with this list in a way that has not been done before. Let's remember where we have been and see where we need to go."

"You are all good questioners.

"You are all good problem finders.

"You are all good analytical thinkers.

"You are all good problem solvers, even for the difficult problems.

"Now we need to take the last step. I want you to become *creational thinkers.*

"What does that mean? It means that you *jump from analysis to synthesis*; from critically evaluating what someone else has handed you to creating something to be critically evaluated by others; from reordering information to creating information. It means forging a path instead of following one. *It means coming up with a whole new kind of cookie.*

"As we try to manage and create with our list of 'oneness,' here are some ideas to keep in mind about creational thinking.

"*Time is on our side.* There is no bear standing in our path, no army attacking our flank, no criminal holding a gun to our head. We don't have to react at all. Many creational thinkers spend a lifetime creating that for which we know and respect them. In fact, most of your heroes made a life's work out of their own personal Game. Earhart, Gandhi, King; their mission was their Game. You may, at some point, find a calling about which you are passionate, and that will become your own life's Game. Even now, when we are just testing this idea with a little Game of our own called 'One,' thought and reflection are more important than speed. For truly creational thought, ideas must flow to you from somewhere beyond the strict limits of your experience. A good baker lets her dough rise all by itself before kneading it into a loaf.

"*Put some sense of order into the confusion of ideas that we have listed.* Without some framework, a jumble of ideas is hard to communicate. You may want to consider several alternative frameworks before you find one that is a best fit.

"*Seek and secure interdisciplinary relationships.* Most people are good at one or two things. They may understand math or plumbing or music or art or science or accounting. A creational thinker needs to understand and use the layering of disparate fields of knowledge to create new links, new bridges, new relationships, and new ways of thinking new thoughts. Consider the first chef who placed an edible flower petal in a salad, the first engineer who encoded ones and zeros on a silicon wafer, the first military consultant who integrated the Tao into a battle plan. These are the creational thinkers. Build bridges of information.

"*Find opportunities in the voids.* Just because we don't hear or see or know that something *is* there does not mean *nothing* is there. Maybe we just haven't seen or heard or thought it yet. The first musician who left a hard-driving four-four rhythm for a half beat of syncopated silence created jazz! Physicists who study the universe find more answers in what we cannot see or detect than in what we can. A Zen master finds self-realization only after he fills his mind with nothingness. Voids are the frontiers, the realm of the under-explored, the under-created, the fertile ground for creation.

"Finally, we need to communicate our creation. It would be a shallow world with a lot fewer heroes if we each could only understand our own awareness of knowledge. Think of all the sensory tools you have at your command that will help us to communicate what we mean by the concepts of 'one' and 'unity.' Remember that experience is the best teacher; if your audience experiences your creative thought in a language that they can understand, you will have succeeded.

"The rest is all a blank canvas. Let's get to work on our Game."

And so it came to be that in the spring, on a warm evening just after the sun went down and crickets filled the still, damp air with their background hum, the Children took to the outdoor stage and performed their Game for the students and parents of the school. I could try to describe it here, in two dimensions and in black and white, but I am neither writer nor poet enough to do so. Games cannot be told; they must be experienced. Their Game was a mixture of sounds and light, of poetry and passion, of theory and inspiration, paints, skits, music, formulas on weathered canvas and plywood backdrops, shadow, movement, old movie clips, modified soliloquies, and tortured prose, each element scripted in a way to convey to the audience the sense of One. Through this stew of sensation, the Children struggled to express to their audience some newly created imagery of what One means. It would be a lie to say that everyone walked away bubbling with the raw success of the Game; many walked away mumbling in confusion, disappointment, or just boredom. But others, some young, some old, some the smartest students, and some at the other end of the grading charts, went home and lay awake in their beds, the full moon streaming chalky white light into the bedrooms, knowing that they would never think of or see One the same way again.

And most of the Children remembered the Game as well. They remembered the struggle to create rather than to manage, to invent from the pure process of mind and experience, to form bridges over the voids with toeholds on the canyon edges of knowledge.

Step 10: In Search of Elegance

If you are out to describe the truth, leave elegance to the tailor.
Albert Einstein

In the beginning our students said that they most valued those people in their lives who best exhibited confidence, vision, happiness, love, compassion, fairness, and patience. We stated that we should be at least equally concerned about teaching the skills of design, invention, exploration, and construction as we are about teaching the stuff of physics, math, history, and literature. Our students recognized this as the twin goals of knowledge and wisdom; as educators we can recognize it as the complementary blend of content and context. They cannot exist independently, and we cannot do our jobs unless we capture both. Content, the nuts and bolts of knowledge, is the foundation of learning. Context, why we bother, is the impetus for the effort.

Our students told us where they want to go, and we have offered the skills to help them advance to that goal. They learned to observe, study, question, analyze, and challenge. They learned that the world is vastly more complex than it was when Mommy or teacher provided nurture and shelter, and that their personal view of that world is integral to their intended outcomes. They learned that problems can be friendly and helpful or nasty and obstinate. And, finally, they learned that, often in the face of failure, a fresh approach or new direction, an undiscovered path, a creational thought, may launch them into the realm of new knowledge or understanding.

What is the goal that I wish for my students? What is the common characteristic of our heroes, the common context which lies at the end of the path? What is the height of the warrior's bar?

I believe it is elegance.

Commonly, elegance refers to a beautiful gown, a memorable dinner party attendant to every trimming, an expensive yet tasteful entryway that welcomes both the guest and the eye, a Mozart sonata. More recently the concept of elegance has become the playground of engineers and software programmers. It helps define their goal of creating an effective and novel solution to often thorny problems with the greatest efficiency.

What is elegance?

Antoine de Saint-Exupery, the French writer and aviator best known for his story *The Little Prince,* states that "In anything at all, perfection is finally attained not when there is no longer anything to add, but when there is no longer anything to take away."

Mathew May, author of *In Pursuit of Elegance: Why the Best Ideas Have Something Missing,* offers some definitions of elegance: "Unusually simple and surprisingly powerful … cuts through the noise, captures our attention, and engages us … achieves the maximum impact with the minimum input." *The Hacker's Dictionary* defines elegance as that which "combines simplicity, power, and a certain ineffable grace of design."

These definitions share the Zen that permeates *The Art of War,* and illuminate why it is both elegant in its own comprehensive simplicity and a guide to achieving elegance. Sun Tzu tells us to do more with less, that winning without fighting is the best kind of victory, that we must conserve energy to successfully engage our opponent, to seem far when near, to seem at rest when most active. Each passage in *The Art of War* is a tactic that builds to a grand strategy of winning not just any victory, but the best possible victory, one that achieves the goal of the state while preserving the army, its resources, and the support of the population.

Sun Tzu says: *In war, then, let your great object be victory, not lengthy campaigns.*

Sun Tzu says: *Hence to fight and conquer in all your battles is not supreme excellence; supreme excellence consists in breaking the enemy's resistance without fighting.*

Sun Tzu says: *What the ancients called a clever fighter is one who not only wins, but excels in winning with ease.*

It is easy to see elegance in the symmetry of the Taj Mahal, in the simplicity of the Mona Lisa, in the looping cables and gentle, arching span of the Golden Gate Bridge, in an Ansel Adams black and white of Yosemite in winter, in the rectangle and touch wheel of the Apple iPod. But we need to help our students and children and employees see the possibilities of elegance beyond the disciplines of engineering, design, programming, and art. Elegant solutions are found everywhere if we allow ourselves to, first, look, and second, not settle for less. But elegance rarely comes easily. Usually it is the end product of years or a lifetime of work, dedication, failure, and recommitment. Thomas Edison famously admitted that he had tried and failed a thousand times to design an incandescent light bulb before he succeeded. Burt Ruttan built dozens of aircraft before Voyager, the picture of elegance in the air, so light and aerodynamic and ethereal that it could fly around the world without refueling.

*   *   *   *

We call smart people "rocket scientists" for a reason: they have to solve incredibly complex design problems, for often unknown or untested conditions, using a minimum of materials in order to limit weight. Faced with the challenge of holding little things in place in the floating environment of zero gravity, they invented Velcro out of little plastic hooks and fuzz. The metaphor of elegant engineering took place during the flight of Apollo 13. Faced with a crippled spacecraft midway from Earth to the moon, three lives hanging in the balance and a world watching, the Houston-based engineers had just hours to figure out how to literally fit a square peg into a round hole using only the materials present on Apollo. Succeed and maybe the astronauts live; fail and the heroes certainly die. The geeks won. That is elegance.

Tiger Woods hooks a drive left of the fairway into a row of trees. His ball lies semiburied in long, wet grass. The green, 170 yards away, lies around a slight dogleg to the left; a low branch takes the direct shot out of play. He has practiced a million different shots a million times, but never this exact one. He takes into account the length and moisture of the grass, the angle and distance to his target, wind, branches, trees, and the advice of his experienced caddy, selects his club, adjusts his stance, invents a shot that has never been played from this spot under these conditions, knocks the ball to within six feet of the hole, and the crowd goes wild. It is an elegant solution to a very tough problem, not one with the consequences of life or death, but supremely relevant within the context of Tiger's world.

It is July 2, 1863, and on a gentle, wooded ridgeline just north of an insignificant crossroads in southern Pennsylvania, Colonel Joshua Chamberlain and the soldiers of the 20th Maine Infantry hold the high ground against several thousand attacking Confederates. Colonel Chamberlain has been told in clear, direct terms that his men form the end of the Union line, and that if the opposing army overruns his position they will flank the Union ranks. He may not withdraw. The battle rages for hours with brutal casualties on both sides. Time after time the 20th Maine repels suicidal charges by the Confederate troops. Finally, the Union soldiers have spent their ammunition, and there is no chance of resupply. Chamberlain assesses his problem and his resources. He can't withdraw, and he can't hold his position without powder and ball. He orders his men to fix bayonets and charge down the slope with the motion of a swinging gate, catching the exhausted Confederate soldiers by surprise and ending the attack. He has designed a solution, one using the only available resources: bayonet, angle of attack, and the exhaustion of his opponent. It likely prevented a major setback, if not outright defeat, of the Union Army at Gettysburg and, given the political pressure on President Lincoln to end the costly war, may well of have prevented the political dissolution of the United States.

In our introduction in the meadow we witnessed a series of artificial dioramas in which normal people were faced with difficult, yet everyday, problems. We are not all rocket scientists or engineers, sports phenoms, or war heroes. The examples with which we started the book were of people just like us, and for each an elegant solution awaits.

The businesswomen may successfully merge two companies, expand into new markets, design new products, and raise shareholder value. The more efficient the solution to their business problem, the more value they can create at the lowest cost, the more elegant their solution.

The priest may help his troubled group of young men to find alternatives to violence. He may not stop every gang conflict, but he may contribute to a marginal decrease in distrust or a small increase in peace on the streets.

The young intelligence analysts may link two or three or a hundred bits of information in ways that would have been overlooked were it not for their ability to recognize patterns or synthesize ideas in a new way. Maybe they pass a critical new twist on to law enforcement, and a terror cell is stopped in time.

The parents of the rebellious teenaged daughter, frustrated as they are, may redouble their efforts to keep the lines of communication open, to let her know how much they love her, to seek advice on those elusive survival skills that every parent needs. They may grow old, look back, and know that they did their best at one of the toughest jobs ever: raising a family.

Elegance is not the province of heroes. It is here for all of us who want to emulate those who we respect, to practice the skills required, and to work hard at it. We must use the tools we have learned, and learn to suffer failure but not defeat.

Importantly, elegance is *not* the sole province of those we respect or revere, of those who share our world view, political party, or side in battle. Elegance deserves our attention not because it is good, but because it is new, creative, and efficient … in other words, because it is *better*. And if we don't keep up with what is better we quickly lose the game, whatever the game may be.

Political and military insurgencies have often been a crucible for elegant thinking, and we must respect them regardless of which side we are on. In the early months of the American Revolution the fledgling American army and associated militia quickly found out that fighting a conventional struggle, massing lines of infantry, marching and firing in step against the vastly more numerous and better trained British regulars and Hessian mercenaries, had limited value. They adopted hit-and-run guerilla tactics, leveraging mobility and knowledge of the terrain, helping to wear down a superior enemy and buying time for training in more conventional warfare.

The North Vietnamese Army and Viet Cong irregulars, unable to move supplies into the south via conventional means due to American air and naval bombardments, built the Ho Chi Minh Trail, a complex web of new and traditional roads, footpaths, and trade routes through dense rain forest, mountainous terrain, and neighboring territory. Initially using men, women, beasts of burden, and ancient rolling stock, and later engaging a sophisticated transportation, communication, and security system, they moved the massive amounts of material needed to sustain their side of the conflict, even in the mud-plagued logistical nightmare of the Southeast Asian monsoon. They used local resources, knowledge of terrain, and traditional routes and relationships to effectively offset the capital advantage of their opponents.

More recently, extremist and paramilitary groups have merged inexpensive and readily available explosives and electronics with easily disseminated information over the Internet to create and sustain mass development and production of improvised explosive devices. IEDs are a perfect example of an elegant solution, one which is driving reactive countertechnology, military planning, and worldwide political decisions. They are cheap, easy to build, use common materials, can be detonated remotely with little risk to the user, are easily hidden, and cause extraordinary damage. They are a nearly perfect weapon of terror or insurgency.

Similarly, al-Qaeda-affiliated extremist groups have adopted and adapted expensive Madison Avenue-style marketing techniques to develop and distribute communication and recruiting videos. The medium has worldwide reach via the Internet. They use a mixture of real news footage and both real and fictional narrative to concoct an extremely compelling and effective argument in support of the extremist jihadist message. They directly target disenfranchised and disillusioned, predominantly young and male, zealots throughout the Muslim world and achieve the goal of sustaining a supply of fighters and suicide participants to the jihad at an absolute minimum of cost or overt coordination. They are an elegant solution to the overwhelming resources of their adversaries that include professional communications and multinational news organizations.

The skills of strategy are our tools in the search for elegance wherever our passion leads us. We see it in our heroes: Gandhi, King, Lincoln, or Earhart; mother, father, favorite uncle, or younger sister; Superman, Wonder Woman, Charlie Brown, or Lancelot du Lac; Obama, Petraeus, or Ho. Unfortunately, the heroes of some are the bin Ladens and al-Zawahiris, and this is just a fact of life. We, too, can overcome difficult obstacles and find or create these unique opportunities that make our lives full, achieve our objectives, and, hopefully, fill the lives of those around us. The key is not wealth or armies, not background or advanced degrees, or even necessarily raw brainpower. The keys are willingness, preparation, openness to new ideas, and the diligent application of strategy.

Elegance is the result of synthesis. The Children designed an elegant performance, using the Glass Bead Game as a model, but turning it to their own interest, the concept of One. By building on a foundation of content, of existing knowledge, they created something completely new in a way that conveyed to their audience a unique and fresh understanding. They applied the resources at hand: their creativity and imagination, a space for performance, the patience of their audience, and probably some props and aids. If it lasted just that length of time and contained just that amount of material to engage but not bore, and if the audience walked away thoughtful if not completely satisfied, then the Children achieved an elegant solution through a synthetic construct based on their previous life experiences. By using content they *created* context.

These examples, and those that surround us every day, are why creational thinking, not critical thinking, should be our ultimate goal in education. Critical thinking is a skill that allows us to steer a valuable course through a known problem. It engages a problem-solving skill set but stops short of what is possible. If problem solving and critical thinking are the goals of education, the bar is too low. Creational thinking, the use of content while branching into the unknown, leads to the possibility of truly elegant solutions. That is where the bar needs to be, particularly in light of the challenges that lie ahead for us.

In our search for elegance, maybe we create something new, or understand something old in a new way. Maybe we fill in a gap of knowledge, fit a new piece into the puzzle of human experience that has been forming for over four million years. Maybe we fail but decide to try again. Hopefully the elegant solutions that tend toward good in the world surpass those that tend toward evil. If we succeed, as scientist, engineer, peacemaker, prophet, soldier, teacher, designer, artist, parent, or just someone putting one foot in front of the other each day in a complicated world, maybe we have become someone else's hero.

*   *   *   *

This path has come to an end. We know that both our successes and our failures have a place in this very real world. I wish that it were not so, that we could construct a model of perfection, a cheap get-rich-quick fad with flawless logic that works for everyone, costs little, and that you can accomplish in your spare time. But that would not be honest, and we would not be falconers.

Have we found all of the answers, answered all of the questions? Are you satisfied? Comfortable? Clear on all points? I hope not. There are no perfect cookbooks for life, but I hope the list of ingredients we have thrown up in the air, and a few ideas about how to mix them, will help lead to less burnt toast and more savory stews.

Over five years, about eighty students participated in The Falconer seminar. For some it was confusing; they were used to being handed intellectual footholds, and in the seminar we were working without a net. For many I think it brought a sense of clarity and focus after twelve years of primary and secondary education that is focused on content more than context. One student, a class salutatorian who went on to study at Stanford, said, as he was recruiting students for the course the next year, "This was the only class in high school that really made me think."

It would be symmetrical to circle back to our morning meadow, to gather all of our players and guides together on a symbolic stage, to thank them and to have them take a bow before mounting up and riding off down that path into the forest where we started. Why not do it, then?

As much as we would like it to, our meadow does not lie on the far side of some Narnian lamppost. We do not get to frolic through the alpine glades of the seventh plane of heaven, at least not yet. Unlike some of our guides and friends, we don't have the weightless luxury of metaphorical construction. We are really here, and there is real stuff that needs doing, and we are going to do it. There are students to teach, mergers to form, terrorists to battle, diseases to cure, theories to unify, fighting gangs to pacify, children to raise. There are games to be played, the rules of which we can only dream about because they belong to their creators before they belong to us. You are that creator because you have come this far on a journey about which you knew little in the beginning. This is the real start of the real path because it is yours. I may have filled in a void or two that existed before I wrote this book, but there are many more voids out there just waiting for the student of strategy and discovery to find and revel in them.

What you do with this is up to you. If you understand *all* of what you have read, there is a pretty good chance you were a falconer or a warrior to begin with. For the rest, perhaps you now see what you have always known a bit more clearly, or perhaps you can put words to a sense of purpose that always resided just below the surface. Perhaps not. If you learned anything new and just once can see a path to solve a personal problem that has stumped you, are better prepared for the unexpected, create a life opportunity that may have been hidden from you, sidestep a battle that does not need fighting, then the journey has been worthwhile. If your children or students learn from Mr. Usher and his Children that there is more to school than math, writing, spelling, history, and science, then they will have a leg up on life that comes from those few special teachers that we all remember so well.

We end with that ferocious passion for the positive that accompanies us through all this hard work. We remember that the answer to "Who cares?" is, "We do!" We are confident that Mr. Usher taught the Children until they were too old for the school, and then he taught more children, because that is what teachers do. More than likely, Mr. Sun and Sunny folded back into their composite, forgave our liberties with the wisdom of millennia past, and awaited the student of strategy who might come knocking. We know that Sunny and Mr. Usher will share many a mushroom hunt and cup of tea in the years ahead.

As for the Children, we hope and expect that they went on to play their own personal games at some point or points in their lives. We thank them for letting us look over their shoulders and for acting as our rhetorical foils. We hope that they remember some of the lessons they learned during their time with Mr. Usher, that their successes are many, that their failures are followed by redemption, and that they, and you, live happily ever after, amen.

Cheat Sheets

Step −1: Who Do I Want to Be?

If we want to grow up to be like the people who we admire, we have to learn much more than math, science, and history.

Without sacrificing your concept of self, the templates of our heroes can help us know where we want to go.

Step 0: Preparation

Happiness doesn't just happen.

Great teachers make us *want* to overcome the challenge of learning.

Each of us may be a *warrior, a general, or a nation*.

The *enemy or opponent* is any challenge, problem, or opportunity to be studied, met, analyzed, or solved.

Battles, military operations, and armed struggles are the process of seeking solutions, overcoming challenges, and creating new ways in which to find the success and happiness we seek.

The land, the terrain, the very contours of the hills and the nature of the ground are the aspects, the characteristics, and the constitution of the problems that we face.

Armies, soldiers, and spies, like knowledge itself, are the tools and skills we each have and use to meet the challenges and solve the problems we encounter.

Victory means finding a solution, a way through the obstacles, overcoming a challenge, the taking of one more unobstructed step down the path towards the life we each desire.

The first task of preparation is to create or take advantage of the opportunity to explore, learn, lead, challenge, or solve.

The second task of preparation is to determine a clear sense of the strengths and weaknesses of the resources at your command.

The third task of preparation is to find a shared basis upon which to communicate.

Step 1: The Art of Questioning

Sometimes answers are dead ends; they don't lead anywhere. Questions are never dead ends.

"What if" questions lead to creative thinking.

If our goal is wisdom, then the process of creating questions and seeking answers may be more important than the questions themselves.

There are times when we need or want to make quick work of a question; there are other times when we want to spend weeks, months, or a lifetime pondering a question as deeply and creatively as possible.

Questions often hide from us like insects under a pile of stones. We have to turn over those stones and find them.

To foster creative thought, jump quickly from question to answer.

If analysis is the goal, slow down, dwell on the answers, and ponder each assumption and each result.

First set a goal. Then ask questions within the scope of that goal. There may be no bad questions, but some can be a real waste of time.

Trace arguments backwards. Question assumptions. Always. It's the only way to prevent garbage in, garbage out.

Resources and abilities are like the arrows in a quiver; the ability and willingness to ask questions are like a long bow. Without the bow, the arrows are just a lot of wood, feathers, and sharp little points.

Step 2: The Boundaries of Subjectivity and Objectivity

Knowledge of self is one of the most important ideas in *The Art of War*.

Sun Tzu says, *So it is said that if you know others and know yourself, you will not be imperiled in a hundred battles; if you do not know others but know yourself, you win one and lose one; if you do not know others and do not know yourself, you will be imperiled in every single battle.*

A person who takes a wholly *subjective* viewpoint believes that all of reality is a function of his or her perceptions. In contrast, a person who takes a wholly *objective* viewpoint believes that things are they way they are no matter who or what acts as the observer.

We at least have to consider the possibility that the subjective view of the world is correct, even for objects and phenomena that seem irrefutably constant.

If we want to understand the world around us, we first need to know ourselves and how that self influences or interacts with the exterior world.

Acceptance that something is possible opens a lot of doors to creative thinking.

Matter, at the foundation level and to the best of our observational abilities, does not exist except as a probability.

At the subatomic level, we cannot objectively and dispassionately observe the physical universe.

Physics demands that the universe is a highly subjective place.

If you start with a passion, whatever it is, and keep asking "why" enough times, almost everyone will arrive at a fundamental point of their worldview that is grounded in faith.

One definition of God is that entity which is omnipresent, omniscient, and omnipotent. Perhaps another definition would be that God is that entity for which true objectivity is reserved.

In order to have complete self-knowledge, the warrior must choose: he and God are one; he and God may some day become one; he and God will never become one; there is no God; he does not know but will seek this knowledge.

The only other option is that he does not care, which is not a valid option for the true warrior.

Step 3: Understanding the System

We analyze systems because we cannot defeat our enemy without first knowing him. The essence of problem solving is designing strategies based on a unique set of relationships posed by the problem itself, as well as a desired outcome.

Sun Tzu says: *Act after having made assessments. The one who first knows the measures of far and near wins—this is the rule of armed struggle.*

We should always be more interested in *why* something is the way it is than we are just in knowing *what* is there.

The Nine Postulates of Understanding the System:

1. First count the arrows in the quivers and the spears in their racks.

2. Next measure the courage of your soldiers, the faith of your people, and the stealth of your spies.

3. The enemy is not known by his portrait at one sitting but by watching and studying him over time, by assessing the ebb and flow of his essence.

4. The good warrior knows the borders of his enemy and does not chase diversions beyond the frontier of his own choosing.

5. To know the whole, the warrior must know its parts; to know the parts, the warrior must organize them; to organize them, the warrior must know his goal, or he is merely shuffling pieces on a board.

6. To fully understand the forest of trees and the braiding of streams, the warrior must understand the forces that bind the one to the other.

7. The wise general knows that the impossible is probably just improbable.

8. Absolute honesty requires the warrior to be more honest and less absolute.

9. The general who shares his vision may find himself at the head of a large army; the general who keeps his vision to himself will likely fight alone.

There are two kinds of people in the world: those who do not believe something is possible until it is proven, and those who believe anything is possible, no matter how improbable. Someone who shares a bit of both points of view is wise.

Step 4: Finding Problems

In order to learn, we have to answer questions. In order to answer questions, we have to have questions to answer. And in order to have questions, it really helps to have problems.

Problems are really just challenges and opportunities in disguise.

Someone who never looks for problems will rarely learn anything new.

Problems are caused by dissonance: the difference between the way something is and the way we want or expect it to be.

Real learning, whether in the classroom or the real world, occurs when an individual takes a personal stake in solving a problem that is meaningful to him or her.

Great teachers do one thing well: they create dissonance in the minds of their students and guide them to a resolution of that dissonance.

Step 5: Solving Problems

The steps of problem solving:

1. Find the dissonance.

2. Articulate the problem.

3. Ask questions; beware the answer that comes before the question is asked.

4. Know yourself; assess your strengths and weaknesses, your resources, or those of your group, before attempting a solution.

5. Know the enemy; understand the strengths and weaknesses of the problem to know its nature.

6. Define the problem in terms of a goal; determine one or more acceptable outcomes.

7. Brainstorm solutions.

8. Understand the implications of possible outcomes.

9. Act; without action all of our work is just so much tacking into the teeth of a nasty gale.

Step 6: When Problems Don't Want to Be Solved

No matter how hard we prepare and try, no matter how well we play the game, there are times and places and systems that defy our efforts at solution. There are problems that don't want to be solved.

Getting to Yes: read the book by Fisher and Urey!

Getting Ahead of No:

- The soldier is trained to fight, not to sign a treaty. To avoid conflict, we must first recognize that it is neither inevitable nor good.

- Paper can be torn by the weakest child, burned by a single match, ripped by even a casual wind. The foundation of working relationships must be mutual interest and, if possible, trust.

- Wolves are known by their howls in the night; armies raise dust over the horizon; storms are preceded by colored skies and seabirds; smoke blows ahead of fire. We must learn to see trouble coming from a distance.

- When attacked, look first for escape. This is not cowardice. We must re-tool our training to value the creative problem solver over the reactionary.

- There is a time for ambassadors and advisors and a time for them to be sent out of the room. Don't let third parties control relationships. Take advice from your counselors, but do the heavy lifting yourself.

- If you win and your opponent loses, you still have an enemy. Win-win solutions to conflicts are good; balanced relationships based on fairness to all parties will prevent conflict from arising in the first place.

- You should avoid narrow defiles where the only path lies between steep walls and a swift torrent. There are many pathways to a solution. If we find ourselves with a single option, particularly one that is dangerous, we have probably, if not certainly, made a mistake in the past.

Battle, in whatever form, is a bad option. No one ever wins. Ever.

But sometimes we have to trash the pretty metaphors, and a warrior is just a warrior.

Step 7: Failure and Redemption

If you deny the essence of your nature, you are not your full self.

To truly consider yourself a warrior, you must set your personal bar very high. If the challenges are not great enough, you either must raise the bar or cease to consider yourself a true warrior.

At some point, you are going to fail in your fundamental goals, your belief system, your moral foundation, your self-view. It is an inevitable result of setting the bar higher and higher.

Redemption comes from trying, despite the sure knowledge that you will fail.

Step 8: The Art of Falconing

Falcons are all of our skills and resources that we have developed and trained, our knowledge and character that we were born with and learned over the years.

Pigeons are the problems and opportunities that we seek out and engage in order to lead a full and productive and happy life.

The responsibilities of the falconer are patience, vision, leadership, and accountability.

The falconer must judge when and how to use his skills; he must know his abilities and their limits; he must be confident that he truly knows the nature of the challenge before he lets his birds go; he must decide if a problem really needs attention; he must practice his skill.

Tactics win battles; generals win wars.

Falcons kill birds; falconers bring home the dinner.

The world just doesn't care, but we do.

Do the best you can because you can.

Step 9: Creational Thinking

We respect our heroes because they help us to see things in a new and sometimes completely unique way.

The creational thinker jumps from analysis to synthesis. It means coming up with a whole new kind of cookie.

Time is on your side. For truly creational thought, ideas must flow to you from somewhere beyond the strict limits of your experience. A good baker lets her dough rise all by itself before kneading it into a loaf.

Put some order into the confusion. A jumble of ideas is hard to communicate.

Seek and secure interdisciplinary relationships. A creational thinker needs to understand and use the layering of disparate fields of knowledge to create new links, new bridges, new relationships, and new ways of thinking new thoughts. Build bridges of information.

Find opportunities in the voids. Voids are the frontiers, the realm of the under-explored, the under-created, the fertile ground.

Communicate your creation. Experience is the best teacher; if your audience experiences your creative thought in a language that they can understand, you will have succeeded.

Step 10: In Search of Elegance

Content, the nuts and bolts of knowledge, is the foundation of learning. Context, why we bother, is the impetus for the effort.

Elegance is the height of the warrior's bar.

Elegant solutions are found everywhere if we allow ourselves to first, look and second, not settle for less.

Elegance is not the province of heroes. It is here for all of us who want to emulate those who we respect, practice the skills required, and work hard at it

Elegance deserves our attention not because it is good, but because it is new, creative, and efficient…in other words because it is *better*.

The skills of strategy are our tools in the search for elegance wherever our passion leads us.

References and Suggested Readings

All quotes attributed to Sun Tzu and *The Art of War*:

"The Art of War", 2007, Borders® Classics. Reprinted by permission. Copyright© 2007 J. W. Edwards, Inc.

Capra, Fritjof. *The Tao of Physics*. Boston: Shambala Press, 1975.

Cleary, Thomas, trans. *The Art of War*. Boston: Shambala Press, 1991.

Fisher, Roger, and Urey, William. *Getting to Yes*. New York: Houghton Mifflin, 1981.

Gardner, Howard. *Five Minds for the Future*. Boston: Harvard Business School Press, 2006.

Giles, Lionel, trans. *The Art of War*. Borders Classics, 2007.

Hesse, Herman. *The Glass Bead Game (Magister Ludi)*. Translated by Richard Winston and Clara Winston. New York: Holt, Rinehart, and Winston, 1969.

Persig, Robert. *Zen and the Art of Motorcycle Maintenance*. New York: William Morrow and Co., 1974.

Pink, Daniel. *A Whole New Mind*. New York: The Berkeley Publishing Group, 2005.

Sizer, Theodore, and Sizer, Nancy Faust. *The Students are Watching*. Boston: Beacon Press, 1999.

Zukav, Gary. *The Dancing Wu Li Masters*. New York: William Morrow and Co., 1979.

About the Author

Grant Lichtman is the Chief Operating Officer of Francis Parker School in San Diego, California, one of the oldest and largest independent schools on the West Coast. Before coming to Parker, he was a principal in several geo-science companies with interests as close to home as southern California and as far reaching as northern Siberia. Mr. Lichtman graduated from Stanford University with a BS and MS in marine geology in 1980 and participated in a number of research expeditions studying the deep ocean basins. He has also been a principal with companies involved with forensic engineering and the development of high school curriculum. He and his wife Julie live in Poway, just north of San Diego. Their son, Josh, is getting his PhD in cellular biology at Stanford; their daughter Cassidy is finishing a BA and MA at Stanford in History and is a volleyball rock star.

Comments and sharing of ideas are invited and may be forwarded to glichtman@francisparker.org.

.

Made in the USA
Lexington, KY
10 October 2014